Understanding BOLIVIA

Vivien Lougheed

Understanding BOLIVIA
A TRAVELLER'S HISTORY

HARBOUR PUBLISHING

Harbour Publishing Co. Ltd
P.O. Box 219, Madeira Park, BC, V0N 2H0
www.harbourpublishing.com

Edited by Ariel Brewster.
Map design by John Lightfoot.
Cover photo of stone chapel and Twin
Sister Volcanoes by the author.
Printed in Canada.

THE CANADA COUNCIL | LE CONSEIL DES ARTS
FOR THE ARTS | DU CANADA
SINCE 1957 | DEPUIS 1957

BRITISH
COLUMBIA
ARTS COUNCIL
Supported by the Province of British Columbia

Harbour Publishing acknowledges financial support from the Government
of Canada through the Book Publishing Industry Development Program and
the Canada Council for the Arts, and from the Province of British Columbia
through the BC Arts Council and the Book Publishing Tax Credit.

Library and Archives Canada Cataloguing in Publication

Lougheed, Vivien
      Understanding Bolivia : a traveller's history / Vivien Lougheed.

Includes bibliographical references and index.
ISBN 978-1-55017-444-1

      1. Bolivia—Description and travel. 2. Bolivia—History. I. Title.
F3315.L68 2008   984   C2008-900011-0

Contents

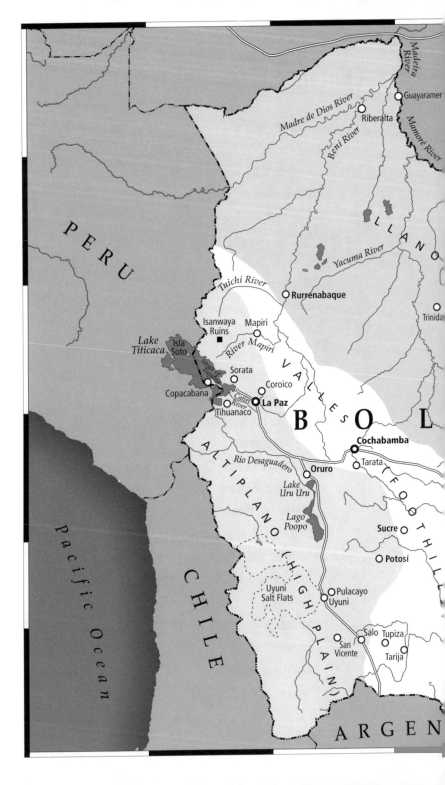

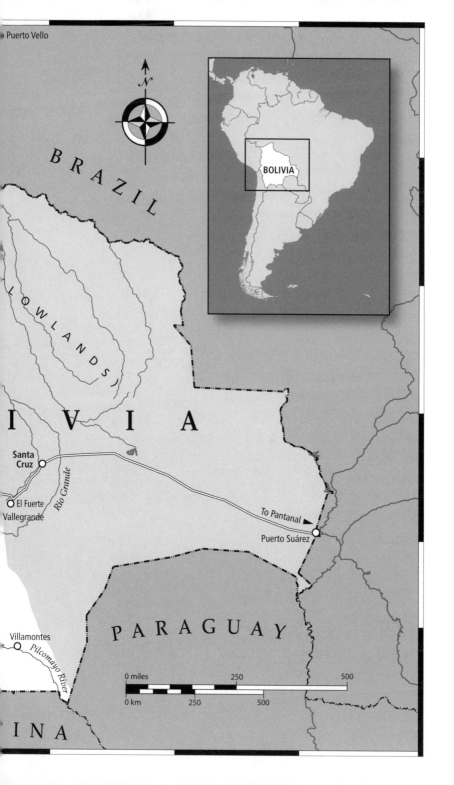

INTRODUCTION

A Traveller's History

A traveller arriving in a new place typically—almost inevitably—starts with promotional history. This is history as seen by patriotic national governments and chambers of commerce. It is a nation's official sequence of celebrated, formative events and episodes, usually dominated by a few charismatic individuals. It tells stories of the sort that will draw everyone, from campesino families to upper middle class westerners and Go Vacations tour groups, to visit the claustrophobic honeycombed tunnels of Potosi, to follow Che Guevara's *via dolorosa* to Vallegrande—riding on horse or donkey right up to the schoolhouse where Guevara was interrogated, photographed and shot—and to gaze at a bronze statue of Simón Bolívar, sword extended, with the simple message on the plaque beneath: *"El Libertador."*

But to learn anything from history, you have to remember it. We travellers are usually non-linear, maybe, with short attention spans, so we remember history by touching it. But we also know that promotional history tends to the simplistic. Just from visiting a few South American countries and following TV news, a savvy traveller would notice, for example, that Bolívar wasn't much of a liberator. He replaced Spanish with Creole feudalism, leaving the Indians in slavery. He started 200 years of government rule by tyrants like Galtieri, Pinochet and Stroessner. Some people may even know that Bolívar regarded himself as a monumental failure. His best line was, "He who makes a revolution ploughs the sea," and you won't see that on any Bolívar monuments.

So my traveller's history starts with the monuments to which the locals have built roads, which they restore, visit and recommend to foreigners who are ready to leave the beaten path. I've included the same explanations and background information that traditional histories find important. But my version of this history tries to get at the drama, the human truth, of history. I'm not going to detail long meetings in stuffy rooms; instead I focus on Bolivia's interesting characters and players. I've organized the history—my "itinerary"—as chronologically as possible, but it's important to know that Bolivia's tumultuous history of conquest and revolt is a tangled and complicated story to tell. And all too often, as you will see, the historical record focusses on the conquerors and not the conquered. With that in mind, the book provides the backstory to Bolivia today.

I first arrived in Bolivia in the late 1990s through the back door, and without any intention of ending up there. I'd been hiking Mount Roraima in Venezuela. We crossed to Manaus, on the Amazon River in Brazil. There were few travellers in Manaus, and those who *were* there were all boating up the Amazon to Peru. The boats were packed.

I'd already been to Peru, so I was looking for something different. I found a captain who was collecting rubber up the Madeira. He had only a few passengers, so he said he'd take us up to Puerto Velho, close to the Bolivian border, for fifty bucks including meals—but we'd have to bring our own hammocks. It sounded like a deal to me, so over an exotic dish of ice cream, I talked my husband John into the trip. Neither of us knew anything about Bolivia.

The vessel chugged up the river, stopping often at villages and hamlets. The men collected rubber and I collected information, photos, fresh fruit and even a parasite. (I'd climbed a tree to pick a lush guava and got the parasite as a bonus.)

We were greeted at the Bolivian border by a friendly official who gave us a warm welcome, three-month visas, and advice on where I could get rid of my now itchy spots. We took a plane to Cochabamba, the recommended city, and I found a doctor specializing in tropical diseases so I could stop scratching and start exploring. We stayed until our visas ran out. But we left unsatisfied—there was so much more to see and we loved the place.

Unless you have tons of time, travelling up the Madeira to Bolivia— our original mode of transport—is not recommended. The easiest and cheapest way to get there is to fly to Lima, spend the night at the airport (Lima is dangerous) and take the 7 a.m. flight to Arequipa. After resting and acclimatizing to the altitude, bus it to the border, which is just half an hour from Copacabana on Lake Titicaca. Peru can be hell; Bolivia is paradise.

Bolivia is a royal banquet of culture, history, landscapes and politics. Prominent celebrity guests over time have included the conqueror Topac Inca, conquistador Francisco Pizarro, liberator Simón Bolívar, revolutionary Che Guevara, torture consultant Klaus Barbie, and desperados Butch Cassidy and the Sundance Kid. Simón Patiño, an impoverished Indian who made a fortune from tin mining and became the richest man in the world, is also here beside the 200 or so Hidalgo presidents, few of who came to power by democratic means. The most recent "celebrity" is Evo Morales, an indigenous Bolivian who was elected president by popular vote in 2005 and went on to snub his nose at America's war on drugs. Dubbed "Evo" by everyone including the press, Morales is a pro-union socialist, and is sometimes referred to as an "uppity Indian" by the Hidalgo establishment who feel threatened by him.

As tourists elbow their way in more and more, they are discovering that all the pleasures of Latin America are epitomized in Bolivia (except, of course, beaches). The graph on the following page shows Bolivia's topographical features and dramatic changes in landscape experienced over short distances.

The flat spot between the two major peaks is the Altiplano, 3,000 metres (10,000 feet) above sea level. The level part far below, between Santa Cruz and Corumba, is the Amazon jungle and Chaco desert, and in between are the foothills and temperate valleys. Towering far above the Altiplano are

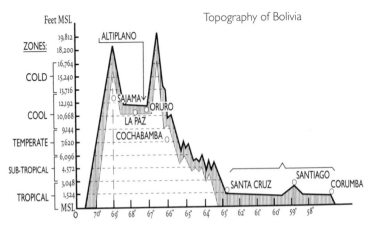

Topography of Bolivia

the glacier-capped peaks of the Andes with the Cordillera Occidental to the left and the Cordillera Real to the right.

These contrasting landscapes feature the Beni, Madre de Dios and Mamoré Rivers flowing into the Madeira, the second largest contributor to the mighty Amazon. Bolivia also boasts the world's highest navigable lake, highest archeological site, highest golf course and highest volcano. Other superlatives include the world's largest wetland, driest desert, richest silver deposit and biggest salt lake. There are ancient Inca and pre-Inca ruins still used for worship by descendants of Atahualpa, the Inca king who was double-crossed and assassinated by Francisco Pizarro during his greed-fest in Peru.

When the Jesuits arrived at Santa Cruz in eastern Bolivia, they were met by Chiquitanos and the less known Guaranis, lowland hunters and gatherers who quickly exchanged their own religion and semi-nomadic life for modern agricultural methods, European classical music and the Catholic religion. The churches they built under the direction of the Jesuits still reverberate with the sounds of 16th and 17th century baroque music. The priests were also met by the Chiriguanos, a warring tribe who migrated into Bolivia from Paraguay in the 16th and 17th centuries to escape from Portuguese slave traders living in the south. The Guaranis were a fierce tribe whose shaman reportedly had supernatural powers obtained by eating the flesh of captured enemy women.

Presently, small pockets of indigenous people live in the Amazon basin and in the Chaco lowlands. These are descendents of tribes like the Chiquitanos and Guaranis that have left little evidence of their existence before colonialism. The Moxos, an Amazonian agricultural group that disappeared around 900 AD, are an exception. They built water-holding mounds used for transportation, growing rice, and developing fish farms. Recently discovered, these mounds are considered by a few particularly zealous tour operators as one of the wonders of the world. Finally, there are still tiny pockets of Guarasug'we, an offshoot tribe of the Guaranis, living their traditional lifestyle in the back acres of Noel Kempff Mercado National Park.

So far as we know, the Andean Altiplano has always housed most of the population of the area now called Bolivia. Electricity, plumbing and modern medical care are often unavailable even today. Mud brick construction methods are used to build homes and temples, and herbal remedies—plus prayer—are administered for all ailments, whether it's a toothache or cancer. The Aymara and Quechua tribes still believe in Manco Capac, the mythological sun god's child who rose out of Lake Titicaca and guided the first Andean people in the ways of survival in their harsh world. Manco taught them to plant crops and care for their llamas—the givers of wool, fuel and food. He taught them how to weave, to build homes and temples, and to fight invaders. He taught them to play the reed flute and *charango*, a string instrument made of armadillo shell, and to dance the *queca*, a scarf dance where the ladies' skirts flew above their knees and the men's dancing slippers flashed faster than the shooting stars so easily seen in the high altitudes.

Today, 60 percent of the nine million people in Bolivia are indigenous, and scholars have pronounced it the most heavily indigenous country in the Americas. Quechua (2.5 million), Aymara (2 million) and Guarani (125,000) are the largest groups. European-Bolivians make up 30 percent of the population. Bolivia has three official languages: Spanish (which is used in business and government), Quechua and Aymara. As a traveller, you will be able to get by using Spanish. Few Bolivians speak English, even those in the tourist industry.

I

PRE-COLUMBIAN BOLIVIA

Tihuanaco

Before the Spanish arrived in Bolivia, the people living in the Altiplano were an advanced civilization. We know this by studying what is left of this civilization, and the ancient city of Tihuanaco ("tee-wan-a-ko") is a good place to start.

While the ruins of Tikal in Guatemala or Machu Picchu in Peru are physically and visually more impressive, the ruins of Tihuanaco are more *suggestive* of a great civilization. Tihuanaco is located on the Altiplano, 70 kilometres (45 miles) west of La Paz, on the road to Lake Titicaca. Archeologists claim Tihuanaco was once on the lake, but that the lake has shrunk over the 2,600 years since Tihuanaco was at its height. Actually, geologists have taken it a step further and believe the lake once covered most of the Altiplano, and the grand salt flats out of Uyuni and Oruro were left as the waters receded.

According to Aymara Indian legend, all life began at the lake. The waters are the tears of the Sun God, Veracocha, who was crying because pumas ate his children. The lake itself has three parts: the north, shaped like a puma, the centre, like a condor, and the area below the Strait of Tiquina, shaped like a man kneeling down to pray. Similarly, the carved deities—still quite visible on the rock at the remote Tihuanacan city of El Fuerte—are also a puma and condor. (In Aymara, "*titi*" means puma or mountain cat, and "*caca*" means rock.)

Covering 6,642 square kilometres (2,565 square miles), Titicaca is 190 kilometres (120 miles) long and 60 to 80 kilometres (40 to 50 miles) wide. The lake averages 100 to 200 metres (325–665 feet) in depth, but is 300 metres (1,000 feet) deep near Isla Soto on the northeastern shore. Twenty-five rivers carry rain and the snowmelt from the Cordillera Real into the lake, and the outflow follows the Rio Desaguadero to the two salt lakes of Uru Uru and Poopo, both located south of Oruro. The surface temperature of Titicaca is only 14°C (57°F), not much for water that has been basking in the sun for over two million years. By comparison, your average swimming pool is 25°C (77°F). But it is a beautiful lake, surrounded by lush hills and sandy beaches, making it a desirable destination for sun worshipers, photographers and boaters. Just don't count on swimming. Remember, too, that at 12,000 feet, tanning is microwaving!

Legend has it that Veracocha, saddened from the death of his children, rose from his lake of tears and created the sun and moon islands so the world would have light. He then made Manco Capac and Mama Huaca, the Aymara rendition of Adam and Eve. Because the lake was so beautiful he created more people and animals so they too could enjoy it. The people built their village, Tihuanaco, on the shores of the lake.

Some archeologists and anthropologists have another version of the origins of the Tihuanacan people: the ruins of Chavín de Huantar, to the northwest of Tihuanaco on the slopes of the Andes in Peru and near the headwaters of the Marañon River, date back to 1400 BC. It is postulated that, due to drought, the people who built Chavín crossed the Andes and conquered, or ran off, those living on the Altiplano. Chavín architectural influence, identified by the use of stone, brick and cement, is found throughout the Bolivian highlands, including at Tihuanaco.

Ceremonial Centre

The ceremonial centre, or the *huaca*, at Tihuanaco was constructed in the 5th century BC by Aymara-speaking tribes who had been living in permanent settlements on the Altiplano for about 3,000 years. The ceremonial centre had outer walls covered with friezes. Some friezes were decorated with gold while others were painted bright colors. The walls were surrounded by a moat and had a number of gates.

Visitors from outlying villages would be clad in finely woven clothes and silver and copper jewellery. Men may have had pan flutes carved from llama bones tucked into their belts, or *charangos* hanging from their shoulders. Their combed hair would have been inspected in a mirror.

From infancy until the age of five children would have worn wooden boards strapped across their foreheads to flatten the soft bone. These boards were four to six inches long and three to four inches wide, depending on the age and size of the child, and were placed on the forehead shortly after birth. Older children, whose skulls were already shaped, would wear hats woven especially to fit their elongated heads. The anthropological museum in Cochabamba is full of such skulls and provides an explanation of how they got that way.

Once near the gates, our imaginary visitor would cross the moat and call to the guards, called *pallapalla* ("pie-a-pie-a"), through a hole in the stone wall. The guards, crowned with headdresses of puma skins, would assess the guest and then give or withhold permission to enter. Visitors today can whisper through the same hole and be heard across the courtyard. Permission to enter is never withheld and silence is consent.

Once inside the walls and through the gate, the visitor would walk across the grounds to the sunken court of Kalasasaya, decorated with stone trophy heads. Anthropologists don't know if they represent sacrificed enemies or the ruling elite. The court is accessed by a wide stairway made from a single block of sandstone that came from a quarry 10 kilometres (6 miles) away.

Other structures at this site are made from 150-ton blocks of volcanic andesite transported about 100 kilometres (60 miles) from various quarries. Tihuanacans used some traditional Chavín masonry, but most construction used a system of interlocking blocks, Lego-like notches and concavities holding the walls together, even through earthquakes.

Also inside the walls is the Gateway to the Sun, a flat arch cut from a single block of andesite three metres by three metres (10 feet by 10 feet). It weighs about 10 tons and is decorated with a human face, condors, and the head of Veracocha, the Creator, holding the staff of thunder in one hand and lightning in the other. He is occasionally called the weeping god because of the tears (representing rain) that run down his face. Besides these three carvings there is a head that appears to be either an elephant, a parrot or maybe—my interpretation—a mastodon. There's yet another carv-

One of the statues made of andesite, a stone quarried one hundred kilometres away.

ing of what could be a hippopotamus or, more likely, a capybara or its smaller relative, the guinea pig. According to journalist Graham Hancock, author of *Mysterious Origins of Civilization*, it is a toxodon, a three-toed mammal that lived in South America from about 1.6 million to 12,000 years ago.

Beyond the Gateway to the Sun is a carved figure, dressed in royal robes, carrying two scepters topped with condor heads. No one knows who this is, though it is probably a king or priest. During spring equinox, which is also Aymara New Year, the sun shines through the gate onto the figure. Even today, priests come to make offerings. Locals always welcome foreigners at these ceremonies. After sunrise during the equinox, the Aymara join in celebration with music, dancing, religious rituals, food, and coca, the sacred leaf of the Andean people still grown, sold and enjoyed by both locals and visitors. They also drink a fermented corn beer called *chicha*.

Not unlike Maya civilizations, the ancient Tihuanacan city was also graced with pyramids; Akapana, the largest, sported seven tiers decorated in gold leaf and red paint. Today, archeologists are still excavating Akapana and visitors are able to see, but not climb it. The Gateway to the Moon is

Gateway to the Sun as it stands beyond the Kalasasaya Temple.

also a large, flat arch, like the Gateway to the Sun, but is far less elaborate (although still impressive). Archeologists have found remains of an extensive
plumbing system that used to run throughout the city, but the few ditches
and clay pipes here and there are not readily noticeable to tourists. What is
most interesting about this is that thousands of years ago the Tihuanacans
had indoor plumbing, but it is an amenity still missing in some Bolivian
homes today.

Life in Tihuanaco

Whoever they were originally, the Tihuanacans lived in a double-tiered class
system: one society for the workers and one for nobility, with each class
governed by their own royalty, judiciary and financial authority. According
to historian Herbert Klein, Tihuanacans had a sophisticated and more advanced level of social organization than any other people in the Americas
at the time. Herding, fishing and agriculture supported both classes. Their
farms splayed out from the ceremonial centre for 600,000 square kilometres (232,000 square miles). Archeologists believe the Tihuanacan culture

did not spread by conquest; none of the cities seem to have been heavily fortified, indicating no fear of retaliation by the conquered.

Archeologists believe there were up to 115,000 residents in the city and another 250,000 in the surrounding countryside. Records show that by 1200 BC they produced fine pottery with anthropomorphic and mythical zoomorphic iconography painted in red, black and orange. The city had gigantic halls with communal kitchens where state-sponsored feasts, often lasting weeks, were prepared.

Their governmental structure was a complicated combination of socialism, democracy and feudalism where a ruling landowner had peasants working for him. The ruling landowner, in turn, provided military service to a ruler or chief. Wealth was distributed equally among the peasants and technological advances were shared, so that wealth increased for all. The peasant classes supplied the nobility with military manpower and agricultural products, and the nobility in turn provided religious ceremonies and government. As stated earlier, they both looked after their own judicial systems.

Farming methods, which produced vast quantities of food, included extensive terracing with some fields stretching 200 metres by 15 metres (600 x 45 feet). They were deliberately layered with a combination of coarse gravel, clay, fine gravel, and, finally, black topsoil, with the clay layer holding water. These fields can still be seen in rural areas throughout the Andes from Ecuador in the north to Tierra del Fuego in the south. For irrigation, the Tihuanacans redirected parts of the Catari River into ditches strategically positioned to get a maximum of sunlight to warm the water. These ditches were also an attractive environment for the waterfowl that Tihuanacans used for food. The warm water also produced algae, a substance used as fertilizer.

A frost-resistant potato, first cultivated around the lake, contained a toxin that the Tihuanacans learned to eliminate by freezing, leaching and sun-drying, thus making the potato not only edible but also rot-resistant. Eventually they developed over 250 varieties of potatoes in varied shapes, sizes and colours. Corn was also preserved by fermenting it into beer. This was done in breweries capable of producing up to 2,150 litres a season.

For another important fertilizer, the Tihuanacans burned puma grass, the spiky clumps of green that grow up to one metre in both height and diameter, and are often seen in uncultivated fields. For heat, they burned llama dung and the high-resin leaves of yareta plants, a high altitude evergreen that resembles moss campion.

Natural Medicines

The Kallawaya, or Aymara doctors, are naturopathic healers, an honoured subgroup dating back to Tihuanaco and maybe earlier. The Kallawalla travelled from Ecuador to Patagonia learning from others, trading in plants and healing. They passed medical traditions from father to son and were exempt from slavery, a custom practised by some tribes in South America. At the age of six or seven a boy was taught how to collect and store plants. He then learned what plants were good for what ailments and he was trained to relate to patients so that he could treat physical and emotional needs. Those practising today know the use of about 300 herbs while specialists know as many as 600. Kallawalla women act as midwives and treat gynecological disorders. For religious enlightenment and under the guidance of a priest, or *yanacona*, royalty snorted willka, ground hallucinogenic seeds imported from the coastal deserts or purchased from Kallawalla. They also used mescaline. But the strongest hallucinogenic, administered as an enema, was extracted from the ayahuasca vine.

Today, Kallawalla still have segregated communities, mostly in the Apolobamba region. During Tihuanacan rule, the Kallawalla spoke a separate language from the ruling and peasant classes, but today they speak mostly Aymara.

Chillata Lake, sitting at 4,226 metres (13,800 feet) and in the shadow of Mountains Illampu and Ancohuma out of Sorata, is a sacred lake where the Kallawalla still hold religious ceremonies. Legend states that the Inca had a palace overlooking the lake and when the Spanish approached, they threw all their gold into the water. Recently, divers have offered to retrieve the gold, but have been refused access by the Kallawalla. Hikers are welcome to explore the ruins along the lakeshore unless a Kallawalla religious ceremony is under way.

Llama Gods

Like the sacred cow of India, llamas were—and still are—the focus of ceremonial life. Cameloids were first domesticated around Lake Titicaca. The Tihuanacans, especially known for their fine weavings made from llama, alpaca and vicuña wool, traded their weavings for fish and foods grown by the lowlanders living along the Pacific coast as far south as central Chile, or as far north as Ayacucho, Peru.

The people of the Altiplano learned to herd llamas, alpacas and vicuñas possibly even before Tihuanaco. Rock paintings near Tarija in southern Bolivia date back 1,500 to 4,000 years, and depict llamas following people. This indi-

Llamas are known to spit green bile when displeased. I can't imagine this cute guy performing such an unpleasant act.

cates that the animals were not domesticated, whereas later paintings show domesticated llamas following on a lead. Some rock paintings near Tarija consist of as many as 200 individual images.

As beasts of burden, llamas made trade between the Altiplano and the Pacific coast possible. Traditionally, at maturity a pack llama was honoured with a *kawra pankara* or llama flower, a string of woven wool, which was attached to the hair on the llama's shoulders and on three consecutive places along its spine. Because they carry larger loads, male llamas were adorned with bigger llama flowers than females and the lead llama was always dressed in a rich head covering. After carrying loads of up to 50 kilograms (100 pounds) for hundreds of kilometres, llamas were rewarded with earrings made from tufts of red sheep wool. One tuft was added for each completed journey. The lead llama was then given corn beer or *chicha*, which was placed in a special bowl called a *kerus*. These bowls were always decorated with a carved wooden llama glued to the centre. Besides sharing the refreshments with their owners, llamas were considered brothers and given family names. The smaller alpacas were regarded as sisters. Today on the Altiplano you will still see these animals rewarded in the same fashion, as always, for the work they do.

Llamas produce milk that can be used whole or processed into a long-lasting cheese. These cheeses, salty and white in colour, can be purchased in any market in any city in the highlands, such a La Paz or Sorata. Although llamas are not raised for meat, after a llama's death the meat is eaten, the leather is tanned and the bones are carved into sharp tools.

During a boy's rite-of-passage at age five—practised much the same today as hundreds of years ago—the child is presented with a special llama-wool cap that he wears during his training. At that time, he is taught to listen to the earth and sun, to walk with the spirits and animals, and to talk to the rocks and wind. The young boy also learns how to collect birds, mushrooms and snails, all lessons essential to survival in the Altiplano.

Centuries ago, llamas were used to drive off diseases. During an exceptionally bad time when the Aymara were suffering from plague and smallpox, they attempted to stop the deaths by loading black llamas with the clothes of plague-stricken people and sending the "scape-llama" (their version of a scapegoat) into the mountains. As the animal ran past, the people christened it with alcohol.

Llama-themed designs are commonly woven into cloth, and weavers and their weavings can still be found throughout the Altiplano and foothills. The Indigenous Art Museum in Sucre maintains the most extensive collection. Look for the Southern Cross pattern, a design based on the most famous constellation in the southern hemisphere. Among the Andean Indians, the four bright stars and accompanying smaller stars represent a mother llama with her young *crea*. You will also see this constellation as a woven pattern on the shawls women use to carry children on their backs. The subtle colours of the wool are obtained using dyes extracted from local plants. Today however, the weavers usually use synthetic dyes because of their availability and low cost.

Ceramic pieces are either designed in the shape of llamas or decorated with llama images that show the animal in the honourable position of carrying deities. Llama figurines of stone, wood, wool, and quinoa paste—contemporary replicas of which are available today in any market—date back at least 3,000 years and indicate something of Andean life during or before the early days of Tihuanaco. The figurines promote fertility, prosperity and downright good luck. During one festival these fetishes are carefully wrapped in woven cloth and buried in special areas in the ground. The following year they are unearthed, washed in *chicha* and rewrapped in clean cloth. Prayers are said and then the fetishes are sprinkled with alcohol and reburied. A very lucky explorer could come across such a celebration, most likely in the Viscachani area of the Apolobamba, and would be welcome to participate in the ceremony.

If a Tihuanacan (or a modern day Andean Indian) wanted his female llama to successfully give birth, he buried a fetish in the corral. In the event that a pregnant llama aborted, the fetus was dehydrated and buried under the corner post of a newly constructed house, thus guaranteeing luck to the inhabitants of the new home. These fetishes, including llama fetuses, can be purchased at the Witches Market (*Mercado de Brujas*) in La Paz. Just don't try to smuggle a fetus through customs in your home country, as it is illegal and the odour would give you away.

El Fuerte

Tihuanacans travelled great distances to the foothills near present-day Samaipata, where they built an outpost called El Fuerte, now the second-largest ruin in Bolivia. Actually, archeologists can't agree which settlement came first, but they do know the two were culturally related.

I personally find El Fuerte more impressive than Tihuanaco because the Inca left their influence by modernizing it, whereas Tihuanaco was deserted by the time the Inca arrived and remained so ever after. Also, El Fuerte is in the dense forest of the lower foothills, not far from Margin de Selva, the beginning of the Amazon and Chaco lowlands, whereas Tihuanaco is in the bleak Altiplano.

El Fuerte's main ceremonial centre is a natural sandstone outcropping, black in colour, 200 metres (600 feet) long, 60 metres (180 feet) wide and

25 metres (82 feet) high with carved triangular, rectangular and trapezoidal niches along the base that held gold-plated statues. The trapezoidal niches are from a later period, after the Inca arrived—the Tihuanacans carved only the triangular and rectangular ones.

On the face of the outcropping is a carved snake representing the underworld. Carved to form a canal, the snake carried blood, water or *chicha* during religious ceremonies. A second carving, a puma, represents life on earth. A photograph taken in 1945 shows the outline of three cats rather than just the one that remains today; images on the soft rock have been eroded by acid rain. The final shape, near the puma, is a condor representing the afterlife. Below the niches are spectators' seats, also carved from stone.

Admiration for the puma and condor is easily understood. The puma is a night hunter who strikes with lightning speed, advancing 7.5 metres (25 feet) in one leap, which makes food gathering appear rather easy. Also, the puma harassed the gods—not even Veracocha was safe. Of the 120 birds that live in the Altiplano, the condor, with its three-metre (10-foot), white-tipped wingspan, is the largest, weighing up to 20 kilograms (45 pounds). Following Indian tradition, Bolivia has made it the national bird. A rather ratty specimen of a stuffed condor can be seen at the park headquarters in Sajama, and occasionally condors can be spotted floating over El Fuerte.

There is no water near El Fuerte, but the porous sandstone, which acts as a sponge during rainy season, saturates with water and seeps it onto the ground to be used during dry periods. If the drought theory is correct, this may have been what kept the inhabitants of El Fuerte alive after those at Tihuanaco died or moved on.

Armageddon

Veracocha was saddened when his people, in their wealth, became sinful and lost faith. He sent the powerful god Khunu to produce a drought and rid the earth of the godless creatures. The lake that once covered the valley all the way to Uyuni shrank to less than its present size, and then started to rise again, as the Inca ruins off the north shore of the Island of the Sun indicate. A few farmers remained in the outlying fields of Tihuanaco while others headed toward the lower lands around Oruro and into the upper reaches of the Apolobamba as the pre-Inca funeral towers (see below) indicate. The Moxos from Trinidad in the Amazon, traditional traders with the Tihuanacans, also disappeared around 900 AD.

Aymara Kingdoms

With the collapse of Tihuanaco and the parallel breakdown of the Waru Empire (700–1100 AD) of Southern Peru, there emerged around Lake Titicaca, over toward Cusco and south across the Altiplano to the salt lakes, a number of Aymara kingdoms. These, for the last century under Inca control, dominated the highlands until the Spanish arrived in the early 1500s. Another prominent culture was the Uru-speaking people, who lived among the Aymara as labourers and who had no social organization of their own. Fortified towns called *pucaras* appeared on hilltops well back from the lake, cameloids were used intensively, and religion was localized. Burial houses called *chullpas* were found in the communities. These burial houses appear in Oruro and the Apolobamba region but are especially prominent on the Kalahuta Islands in Lake Titicaca.

Kalahuta Funerals

Surrounded by tortora reeds, the Kalahuta Islands are inhabited by people living in stone houses with straw roofs. These people are probably ancestors of the Tihuanacans. From 1200–1550 AD, the islands were used as cemeteries and had numerous *chullpas*. These circular stone burial towers stood about three metres (10 feet) high and 2.5 metres (8 feet) wide. Some of these are still visible today. Because of their age it is assumed the Inca adopted *chullpas* from the locals. Each tower contains the corpse of a prominent person, called a *mallku* ("may-koo"), and buried with him is usually an animal-shaped vessel. The tower doors face west toward the setting sun, representing the end of life. This location allows the spirit to leave and continue on its journey to wherever spirits live. It is believed that if you remain on the west side of the island after dark, the spirits will steal your soul and leave your body dead, spiritless or mindless. If you try this, please inform me of the results.

Because the island was once under water, fossils and snail shells can be found embedded in the rocks near the towers. The shells are well above the

Stone hut used by the Aymara and Quechua living in the high Andes.

recently rising high water levels, thus indicating that Titicaca was higher, and consequently covered a larger portion of the Altiplano. Also interesting is that many of these marine organisms are saltwater shells, suggesting that the area was once part of an ocean and may have become separated during a continental shift.

Chullpas near Oruro and in the Apolobamba vary in design, with some standing 40 metres (120 feet) high. They are constructed from small rocks or ground and polished boulders like those found in Sillustani, Peru, near the Bolivian border. Still others are of adobe brick, with the doors facing east rather than west—no one knows what this indicates.

2

THE INCA

Lake Titicaca

According to native legends, the Inca civilization began with a white-skinned tribe that migrated to Cusco from Lake Titicaca, possibly the same white-skinned people created by Veracocha. Some anthropologists believe the Inca came from the high Peruvian Andes above Cusco and subjugated the more numerous Quechua, yet adopted their language and religion. Still others claim that an especially aggressive Quechua tribe, who called themselves and their rulers "Inca," came from the hills and conquered the area. Whatever happened, it occurred around 1400 AD.

After the Inca built a strong administrative centre at Cusco, they migrated north to Ecuador and Colombia, south to Central Chile and Argentina and through the Bolivian Altiplano, known then as Kollasuyo ("koy-a-soo-yoe"). The empire was linked by all-weather stone roads with suspension bridges spanning the canyons and rivers. On these roads, runners carried messages 200 miles within two days—faster than Canada Post in the 21st century! Granaries were built in productive areas to store corn and other food for times of crop failure. The Inca extended and improved the

Tihuanacan system of terraced fields and irrigation channels, and they built and manned forts and sentinel posts.

Most tourists are mightily impressed by the Inca, and I'm among them. One North American traveller I met on the Island of the Sun told me he wished he'd been there to meet Columbus with a machine-gun when he landed, to prevent the Americas from being conquered. Feelings are strong, which says something about us. Perhaps many travellers, most of whom are Europeans or North Americans of European descent, identify with the Inca because we are like them—expansionists, colonizers and bureaucrats. We see them as feathered Romans.

The Aymara remained autonomous, preserving their customs, social organization, language and religion. They worked as well-paid miners, construction labourers and soldiers for the Inca. The population of the empire, in the relatively short 100-plus years of its existence, was about twelve million. Spain at the time had six or seven million.

Vacation Islands

As the economy prospered, the islands on Lake Titicaca became important pilgrimage resorts for the rich. The Island of the Sun, where Veracocha is believed to have created Manco Capac and Mama Huaca (the founders of the Inca Empire), became a most sacred destination. Here, visitors can see a rock carving of the bearded Veracocha sitting next to a puma. Although a lot of imagination is needed to discern the image, the donation box under it, where Inca left *chicha*, is very clear.

Chincana, a village at the north end of the Island of the Sun, means "a place to get lost." The village was

Vivien at Chincana. In Inca times, the offshore island in the background was part of a group of three islands used by rich visitors. Treasures have been found in the ruins there.

mainly workers' quarters, but it still has an impressive labyrinth of passages, hiding places and rooms with false doors (which to me suggests intrigue and mystery rather than a resting place for servants). At the entrance to Chincana is a sacrificial table where human and animal hearts were left to thank and appease the gods for whatever reason, be it drought, floods, sickness or prosperity. Today, Aymara guides encourage visitors to rub the table and extract enough energy to hike to the far end of the island in time to catch their boats back to the mainland.

Hikers are encouraged to rub this ceremonial table to extract energy so they can get to the other end of the island in time to catch their boat back to Copacabana.

Chincana overlooks the four tiny resort islands of Chullo, Koa, Pallalla and Marka Pampa—all just offshore and now mostly under water. The structures on these islands were obviously built when lake levels were lower. During excavations on Marka Pampa in 1992, Archeologists found a carved stone box containing a medallion, cup and puma replica, all exquisitely designed in gold. The box was so well crafted that the contents remained dry despite being submerged for centuries. Since then, the islands have revealed a city of pathways, a protective stone wall, and more stone boxes filled with treasures.

The most impressive item from the first box found was a clay carving of Ekeko, a moustachioed man wearing a poncho and carrying baskets. Considered the God of Abundance, Ekeko bestows fertility, happiness and prosperity on those who honour him. He is now housed in the island's museum, which was closed at the time of writing due to infighting between locals. Apparently, it will reopen once they come to an agreement about management. If not, they may revive the traditional practice of pushing enemies into the lake as an offering to Panchamama (Mama Huaca), the earth goddess.

Nunnery

As the islands became overrun with vacationers, the Inca moved their religious centre and nunnery to the Island of the Moon, a half-hour boat ride from the Island of the Sun.

The Island of the Moon is a mere three kilometres (5 miles) long and barely one kilometre (0.5 miles) wide, and represents the female counterpart of the sun. The island's nunnery held the virgins of the sun: women who, because of their beauty, were dedicated to the gods and did little more than make *chicha* and weave cloth to be used for religious ceremonies. The island was called Coati, which, according to some linguists, means "the place for elected women."

From studying the ruins anthropologists have learned that the religious centre, resembling a palace, was constructed in typical Tihuanacan architecture, but the doors were of Incan design—suggesting the building was used by both cultures.

In more recent years, from the 1930s to the 1960s, the island was a prison for political dissidents. (As you will see, Bolivia has had plenty of these.) By 1930 there was little left of the nunnery and its adjacent palace, but the prisoners were forced to reconstruct the 35-room nunnery using the original stones found scattered around the site.

Navigation

Tortora reeds grow along the shores of Titicaca, and it was only natural that the Tihuanacans and Inca would utilize those materials to built reed boats. (Actually, because the reeds decompose within a short period of time, there is no physical evidence of this, nor are there rock paintings depicting the reed boats. But using records from early explorers and priests, historians have been able to discern this information.)

Tortora reeds belong to the papyrus family, grow two or three metres (6.5 to 10 feet) above water level, and are used for construction of traditional boats, houses, musical instruments and furniture. They are also used as fodder. Visitors can watch boat construction onshore at Siquani on the Yampupata Peninsula, a few hours' walk from Copacabana, or they can go to Suriqui Island to actually partake in making boats, as did Norwegian

Tortora reed boats, like the one used by Thor Heyerdahl during his Kon-Tiki expedition, require over a million reeds to make and at 15 metres (50 feet) long, weigh 15 tons before being put into the water.

adventurer Thor Heyerdahl. He built his own reed raft for his famous Kon-Tiki expedition, an amazing 7,000-kilometre (4,300-mile) trip from Lima to a reef in the Tuamotu-Gambier Archipelago in Polynesia, in 1949. Heyerdahl was attempting to prove that people could have arrived in the Americas via reed boat before the Asians travelled over Beringia, the Bering land bridge.

A standard reed boat 15 metres (45 feet) long by five metres (15 feet) wide and two metres deep (6 feet) weighs 15 tons when dry. Its construction requires 1.5 million reeds, which sop up water and gain more weight when in the lake. The gondola-shaped reed boats built by the Inca were decorated with a puma or other fierce animal at the bow to protect the sailors from danger.

Reed roots are planted in the spring in muddy water close to shore, and are harvested for the first time the following October (and then three times each year after that). During the harvest, reeds are cut 1.5 metres (4.5 feet) below water level. It takes four to six weeks for the reeds to dry. If left unharvested, reeds eventually grow wild and form small islands that then become habitable.

Above: In Tihuamaco a wall is imbedded with enemy heads at the sunken patio of Kalasasaya Temple.

Left: The Gateway to the Moon in Tihuamaco is still used for ceremonial purposes during the spring and fall equinox.

The doors of funeral towers in Apolobamba face west toward the setting sun, representing the end of life and allowing the spirit to leave and continue on its journey to wherever spirits live.

Niches located on the south side of the ceremonial rock are triangular, rectangular and trapezoidal. Only the trapezoidal are Inca designs.

Opposite: Hikers on Isla del Sol try to finish the four- or five-hour hike in time to catch their boats back to Copacabana.

Llama fetuses (beneath table) are sold in the witches' market. For good luck, fetuses are placed under the corner posts of new buildings.

The original painting is still visible on the walls of San José de Chiquitos.

Above: The potato was first cultivated in the Andes. Today there are over four thousand varieties world-wide. Here, nine types are for sale.

Left: The church steeple in Sucre, often called *La Ciudad Blanca,* the White City.

Vicuñas were hunted almost to extinction for their soft wool and tender meat. This protected herd, near Sajama, has increased to about 9000 animals.

Stations of the cross on the "Christian" hill overlooking Lake Titicaca. The summit of the hill is also used by Kallawaya medicine men for religious ceremonies.

These flats contain ulexite, a mineral used to manufacture borax as well as fertilizers and enamels for ceramics and glass.

A storm on the Beni River, which flows into the Madeira and continues to the Amazon.

Overleaf: Just out of Potosi, these experienced local hikers guided the author to shelter when they heard a dangerous hailstorm coming over the pass.

The Mainland

The Inca vacationed on the islands and around the shores of Lake Titicaca in the same areas once central to Tihuanacan civilization. Ochre paintings of the Inca flag are still visible today on a wall overlooking the lake, just out of Copacabana toward the Peruvian border. Above the flag are bathing pools used by those unable, or not wanting, to go to the islands. It is still possible to see how rainwater flowed down the surface bedrock at the top of the hill, along ditches and down into the hand-carved rock tubs, through openings in the tub walls, and from one shallow tub to the next. It is possible that rocks and mud were used to block or redirect the flow and fill the pools. Below the pools and around the side of the hill, visitors will notice a flat rock face with two bright, rust-coloured seams of rock forming arches. Here, marriage ceremonies were performed.

Across the valley from the wedding rock is the Inca tunnel, believed to go through the mountain and under the lake to Pilcocaina, a town at the west end of the Island of the Sun. The entry to the tunnel is paved with river stones, but present-day Inca warn foreigners not to enter. If you do, insanity is guaranteed. This was proven (I was told) when an earthquake caused rocks to come loose and hit a local man on the head. He instantly became crazy, never to be cured.

Along the road from Copacabana to La Paz are carved seats of the sun, which were once used for council meetings. The stone niches held gold-covered figurines, but the abstract designs carved onto some of the rocks require imagination to decipher. Some believe the large stones represent mountains and contain the souls of the dead. Near the seats is a throne, presently used by Aymara priests during the winter

Local Aymara, Sonia and Oscar, stand on a paved Inca road.

Horca del Inca or Intiwatana is believed to be an astronomical observatory for the pre-Inca. During the winter solstice in June, a single beam of light shines between the peaked rocks on the right and covers the lintel.

solstice. Beyond the throne is another set of natural spring baths once used by visiting kings.

Intiwatana, the hill north of Copacabana, was used as an astronomical observatory by Inca and pre-Inca. In 1978, Oswaldo Rivera from Bolivia's National Institute of Archeology discovered that, in the first hours of morning during the summer solstice, the sun illuminates a stone crossbeam set on two stone pillars about four metres (12 feet) high. During winter, a single sunbeam lights only the centre of the crossbeam, indicating the accuracy of their yearly measurement of time. Remnants of stone walls, still visible on the hill, separated sacred areas from public ones.

Apolobamba and Expansionism

North of the lake in the Apolobamba region, the most isolated and rugged Andean mountain area in Bolivia, are the 500- to 800-year-old Iskanwaya ruins, clinging to the edge of a cliff hundreds of feet above the Llica river. Although the exact dating is questionable, it is believed that the ruins were trading outposts where Inca exchanged goods with people living farther east, including a few tribes from the upper Amazon.

The Iskanwaya ruins were found in 1913 by Erland Nordenskiold, a Swedish anthropologist, and his wife Olga. They concluded that it was the fortress of Cuscotuyo, which is mentioned in the journals of the Spaniards Sarmiento de Gamboa during the late 1500s and Bernabé Cobo in the mid-1600s.

These journals claim there were three fortresses in all: Dilava, Conyma and Cuscotuyo. In 1994 two Finnish archeologists, Ari Siiriäinen and Martti Parssinen, found all three and surmised that Iskanwaya was definitely one of the three. However, there are other forts along the north shore that may have been part of a chain of fortresses and trading centres.

At one time Iskanwaya had 75 buildings made of slate, mortar and mud, decorated inside with gold carvings and ceramic pottery from the Mollo culture, a subgroup of the Tihuanacans. The residents also built huge aqueducts leading to holding ponds. The water was used mainly for agriculture.

Inca Organization

The Inca were brilliant administrators. They formalized what the Quechua and Aymara already had—trade routes moving textiles, metals, meat and dried tubers from the Altiplano to the coast and foothills. They brought corn and fish from the coast, and corn, coca, quinoa, fruit and wood from the foothills. An efficient taxation system supported large contingents of soldiers and officials and paid for the infrastructure. The army was impressive, quickly massed and well armed.

But this organization was designed for settled agricultural areas. The lowland hunter/gatherers of the Amazon and Mamoré tribes put a quick halt to further expansion in their direction, though the empire probably would have moved south and east through the foothills, onto the plains and high valleys, and into what is now Argentina. These limits to expansion are no reflection on the Inca military; not even the Spanish could take the lowlands. Some of the indigenous tribes, highly skilled in guerilla warfare, survived with their social organizations unchanged into the 20th century.

End of the Empire—Pizarro Arrives

Unless you decided to fight them, the Inca were benevolent rulers, allowing their conquered people to live as they always had, using their own language and religion. In turn the conquered were hired for labour at fair wages. The Inca expected the same courtesy when and if others conquered them. This, it turned out, was a weakness.

After the famous Massacre of the Aztecs in the Main Temple in Tenochtitlan in 1520, Herman Cortez, the Conquistador of Mexico, became tutor to his second cousin Francisco Pizarro, the illegitimate son of a low-ranking soldier. From Cortez, Pizarro learned how to defeat local populations.

Meanwhile, Alonso de Ojeda, who accompanied Columbus on his second voyage, was earning the reputation of being a harsh and vindictive soldier. Ojeda took Pizarro and Cortez to Hispaniola, the island presently known as the Dominican Republic and Haiti, where he showed them some new tricks in torture, deceit and killing. Impressed with his teacher, Pizarro continued travelling with Ojeda to San Sebastian on the eastern shore of the Darien (Panama). After learning all he could, Pizarro left Ojeda and crossed the Isthmus of Panama with Vasco de Balboa. Pizarro spent a few years as a pig farmer in Panama, but that must have been boring and certainly far less lucrative than taking gold from natives. During the 1520s, he started exploring the west coast of South America.

While Pizarro was learning the ways of a conquistador, Huayna Capac, leader of the Inca in Peru, fathered two sons: Atahualpa, a bastard, and Huascar, the legal heir. In 1523, as he lay dying from smallpox, Capac divided his empire between the two. This didn't sit well with Atahualpa. Civil war broke out.

After receiving financial help from an influential priest named Hernando de Luque and the blessing of Charles I, King of Spain, Pizarro and another conquistador named Diego de Almagro purchased and outfitted ships and soldiers. They set sail and arrived in Lima in 1531.

Shortly after Pizarro arrived, Atahualpa defeated and imprisoned his half-brother, Huascar. Atahualpa declared himself king but failed to consolidate his power with the people. It was a perfect situation for the gold-hungry Pizarro to take over. The Inca were already divided and ready to be used against one another. Most historians believe smallpox was the advance column of the Spanish conquest of the Americas, but recent studies conducted by historian/professor Robert McCaa from the University of Minnesota challenge that theory.

Estimates of the number of people living in the Americas when Columbus arrived vary wildly, from 8.4 million to 112 million. The latest belief is that there were about 50 million all together, with 12 million belonging to the Inca Empire. My sources say that by the end of the 16th century—just about 100 years—80 percent of the indigenous population had died. Mexico, for another example, began the century with about 25 million people but was reduced to one million by the end of the 1600s due to war, destruction of crops, harsh labour conditions and disease.

Pizarro's most notorious act occurred on November 16, 1532, when he met with Atahualpa at his camp in Cajamarca, located about 750 kilometres (450 miles) northeast of Lima. Five thousand Inca came unarmed. Not one Spanish soldier was visible. A Quechua translated while a priest read out the *requerimiento*, a document the king required soldiers to read to people before conquering them.

After reading the document, the priest handed Atahualpa a bible. Understanding the request for submission, Atahualpa hurled the book onto the ground in contempt. Pizarro's hidden army—armed with shields, heavy metal swords and a few guns—then attacked, killing about 2,000. The surviving Inca retreated and armed themselves as best they could with bows and arrows and spears headed with sharpened stones. Their "protective shields" were made from cloth and leather. It must be remembered that Inca were a peaceful people for the most part, so keeping a military equipped with advanced weapons was not their forte.

The Spanish took Atahualpa prisoner, but he was imprisoned in comfort, as was the right of captured nobility according to Spanish law. As Atahualpa lay in prison, the soldiers sought out and killed his brother, Huascar—under the orders, some suspect, of Atahualpa.

It didn't take long for Atahualpa to realize that the Spanish loved gold above all else, so he cut a deal, promising to trade a room the size of his prison cell full of gold and a second full of silver in exchange for his life.

Pizarro agreed and Atahualpa had messengers bring the bounty. According to some historians, it was 6,100 kilos (13,420 pounds) of 22-karat gold and 12,000 kilos (26,000 pounds) of pure silver. The Spaniards couldn't believe their luck. Each foot soldier received 20 kilos (45 pounds) of gold and 40 kilos (90 pounds) of silver while Pizarro hauled away 285 kilos (630 pounds) of gold and 575 kilos (1,265 pounds) of silver. But Pizarro didn't keep his part of the bargain. After receiving the treasure, he charged Atahualpa with inciting treason and had him sentenced to death. He was given the option of being burned at the stake or baptized and strangled. Atahualpa chose strangulation.

The death of Atahualpa was a bad move for Pizarro, as he lost the trust of the Indians. He knew from Cortez and Ojeda to act quickly, however. He captured Cusco, located 400 kilometres (250 miles) north of Lima, had the Indians tortured, and then stripped the tombs, palaces and temples of their treasures. He made Manco Capac, the younger son of Huayna Capac, a puppet ruler, but soon had him killed too. This final act solidified the Indians' distrust, and they again rebelled. One advantage the Indians had over the Spanish was that some spoke Aymara, a language not understood by any of the Spanish interpreters. The Indians were able to make their battle plans in Aymara without detection. Today, the Aymara pride themselves with this honourable contribution to the past.

Meanwhile, Pizarro's partner Almagro led an army south, past Lake Titicaca and through western Bolivia into Chile. He found Chile's central valley to have a pleasant climate, but no gold or silver. Instead, he was met with heavy resistance from the Araucanian Indians, so he returned to Lima to help Pizarro, who was busy putting down rebellions by murdering thousands of Indians.

Once the Indians were subdued, Pizarro and Almagro couldn't agree on territorial rights. In 1538 and within two years of Manco Capac's death, Pizarro, feeling threatened by his compatriot, had Almagro executed. Pizarro then kept tight control of his conquered subjects across an expanse that included most of present-day Peru and Bolivia, then known, respectively, as Lower and Upper Peru.

In Upper Peru, Pizarro built an administrative city at the Indian village of Choke-Chaka, later called Charcas, then Chiquisaca, then La Plata, and finally Sucre after the second president of Bolivia and Simón Bolívar's greatest general. When Captain Pedro de Anzures arrived in 1538, he bastardized the Indian name to Chiquisaca, meaning Golden Gate, although the official Spanish name was Ciudad de la Plata de la Nueva Toledo. One of the big attractions was the newly discovered Porco silver mine, located about 100 kilometres (60 miles) farther up the Cordillera Real in a volcano between the Indian village of Potosi and the town of Pulacayo. Pizarro's brothers Hernando and Gonzalo settled in Sucre and plucked another ton of loot out for themselves.

Within three years of Almagro's death, Almagro's mestizo son Diego (called El Mozo to distinguish him from his father) snuck into the palace and executed Pizarro. His burned bones were shipped down to Lima and eventually entombed in the cathedral's basement crypts. The year was 1541, just nine years after Pizarro attacked and killed Atahualpa.

Taki Onqoy Revolt

Shortly after the conquest, the Indians decided that the Spanish gods must have been looking after the Spanish, and that their own Indian gods were angry with them for neglecting their feasts, fasts and offerings. They tried to reconnect with the past by forming the Taki Onqoy society. The name translates to "dance of disease" or "dance of desperation." Members rejected Spanish food, gods, clothes and names, and they especially opposed women having sex with priests. The movement gained momentum until 1565, when a huge revolt led by Inca Titu Cusi was planned in the villages around Cusco. The Spanish negotiated a rocky peace that lasted until they could find an official reason to attack. That reason came in 1572, from the Catholic Church, when the Inca were charged with idolatry (worship of their own gods) and heresy, and then imprisoned or killed.

During that same period, Túpac Amaru I, the legitimate and educated son of Manco Capac II, became king and openly opposed the Spanish by destroying churches. He was captured along with his pregnant wife after a battle at Vilcabamba, Peru. They were marched back to Cusco and sentenced to death. Ten to 15 thousand Inca gathered in the plaza and watched as

Túpac's tongue was cut out, his wife and six-year-old son were dismembered and, finally, his decapitated head was impaled on a lance near the gallows.

A sigh of sorrow was heard from the crowd and then silence. Túpac's death temporarily took away the Inca's overt fighting spirit and members of the Taki Onqoy, afraid of more reprisals, disbanded. But effective Indian resistance rose again. The Chiriguanos stopped European expansion at the Gran Chaco until the mid-1600s. The society again surfaced when the Indians held La Paz under siege in 1781 (see Chapter 5) and then joined Bolívar during his Independence Wars. And Almagro's old enemies, the Araucanians, weren't subdued in Chile until the end of the 19th century.

3

SPANISH BOLIVIA

End of the Conquistadors

On the way to Chile in 1535, the Almagro expedition marched through the Lake Titicaca and Altiplano regions of what is now Bolivia. There was little resistance. The area had been loyal to the Huascar faction during the Inca civil war and welcomed the large number of Huascar-loyal Inca troops. The Spaniards were too busy fighting among themselves in Lower Peru to pay much attention to Upper Peru. That changed in about 1545, when Cerro Rico, a silver mine near the Indian village of Potosi, went into production. It turned out to be the most lucrative silver mine in the world, and the silver passed through La Paz by the shipload. As the conquistador families and the newly established viceroys struggled for control of the Andean outback, the infighting raged on.

For a quick summary: conquistador Diego de Almagro seized Cusco in 1537 and made himself king, which resulted in civil war. The following year, Diego de Almagro was killed by conquistador Hernando Pizarro. Almagro's son El Mozo inherited his father's position. In 1541, El Mozo killed conquistador Francisco Pizarro. The following year, El Mozo was captured and killed by Vaca de Castro, a special investigator for the King of Spain, and in

1544, Blanco Núñez Vela became the new viceroy of Peru. He passed numerous Indian liberation laws that were unpopular with Gonzoles Pizarro, who in turn—with the help of another conquistador Francisco de Carvajal—defeated Núñez in 1546. That same year, Pedro de la Gasca became the new viceroy of Peru and repealed the laws passed by Núñez. In 1548, Gasca captured and killed Gonzoles Pizarro.

But Gasca showed mercy at Gonzoles's death. He explained, "His head was sent to hang in a cage in Lima; his home in Cusco destroyed and the earth about it salted. My generals insisted that he should be drawn and quartered but I demurred out of respect for the late marquis, his brother."

Administrative Structure

By the 1560s the southern and eastern borders of Bolivia were roughly established. Spanish conquistadors from Buenos Aires had taken Paraguay, and their army of Spanish and Paraguayan Indian troops had settled into the Santa Cruz area. The warring Chiriguano Indians successfully fought off the Spaniards and pushed westward, cutting the Lima/Sucre-based Spaniards off from Argentina.

The viceroy at Lima turned his main managerial focus toward Potosi. For Upper Peru, Lima was the port, Sucre the administrative centre, La Paz the major link to the sea and a big supplier of labour. The foothills provided wheat and cattle. The Yungas produced fruit and, most important to the miners, coca.

Chiquisaca/La Plata/Sucre

Sucre, also known as La Plata or Chiquisaca, eventually became a white colonial city sparkling like a diamond in the surrounding brown mountains. In 1559 the city was proclaimed the centre of the Audencia de Charcas, an independent royal court with judicial and executive powers presided over by a judge and independent of Lima. The territory included parts of Peru, Bolivia, Paraguay, Chile and Argentina.

Because Potosi was the financial powerhouse of South America, the King of Spain made sure it was well—or at least efficiently—managed. But the managing officials wanted a gentler climate at a lower elevation in which to live, so they built mansions in La Plata. This way they could still conduct necessary administrative duties and make money from the mines in Potosi while enjoying the eternal spring climate of La Plata.

One of the oldest buildings in Sucre, the Casa Libertad (government house), is located on the plaza and was built in 1621. Initially it was a convent for the Jesuits, but after their expulsion in 1767, it became home to the first university in Bolivia and the third in the Americas, with the University of Mexico (1551) being the first and the University of San Marcos in Lima (1551) being the second. Bolivia's university was called the University of San Francisco Xavier and opened its doors in 1624 for the purpose of training religious leaders.

Potosi Period

Once a sleepy village tucked into the high folds of the Cordillera Real and 150 kilometres (95 miles) from the present capital of La Paz, by the mid-1500s Potosi had become the site of the greatest mineral discovery in all history. Its wealth both sustained and rotted the Spanish Empire. *Vale un Potosi,*" a phrase made popular during that time, translates as "it's worth a Potosi," and still resonates today.

The peak of Cerro Ricco is visible beyond the tiled rooftops of Potosi.

Potosí is shadowed by the impressive Cerro Rico, also known as Sumaj Orko in Quechua, or Rich Hill in English. The mountain stands at 5,183 metres (17,000 feet) above sea level. Cerro Rico is one league, or 5,572 metres (18,300 feet), in circumference and is finely netted with roads and trails leading to the mine shafts that reach down to the world's richest silver deposits.

There are many variations of the Cerro Rico discovery story; the date is particularly debatable. By some accounts the Spaniards had started trickling silver out by 1540 and the mine was in full operation by 1545. The most popular version of the story dates from 1544, and involves a stubborn llama travelling with his owner, Diego Huallpa, from the Pacific back to his mountain village. Along the way, Diego's animal became tired and lay down in typical llama fashion, refusing to move. Knowing it was hopeless to try to push on, the herder made camp, had supper and slept. In the morning he found his pot had welded to a hard substance that had accumulated in his fire pit. The substance was silver. The first flaw in this great story is that silver melts at 370°C (700°F) to 480°C (900°F), a much higher temperature than wood or llama-dung fires can produce. The second flaw is the date—the Spaniards had been extracting silver there since 1540.

Hearing of Huallpa's find, an Inca chieftain from Quito examined the silver and was so impressed with the quality he decided to mine the mountain and have jewels made for his court. Just as his workers began digging, a Quechua god thundered, "Do not dig, the silver is meant for others." The chieftain left the mountain.

The story continued to circulate. On April 10, 1545, the Spanish moved in and established an official village called Villa Imperial de Carlos V after their king. They named the first mine La Descubridora (the discovery). Within two years, the population of the village grew from a mere 170 Spaniards and 3,000 Indians to 14,000 people. By 1630 it had swollen to 160,000, making it more than half the size of London, England, at that time.

Holy Toledo

From 1540—the first trickles—to 1560, when the silver was gushing, the richer surface deposits were stripped from the hill. The Spanish deepened their control of the Indian population, allowing the Aymara extended-family agricultural settlements to run themselves as the Inca had done, while creaming off taxes in the form of agricultural products and labour. The taxes paid for the army, administration, and enforcement of family law and for priests to "culturally refine" the Indians at schools.

After 1560, the miners had to go underground, which was far more expensive. The deeper ore was also less concentrated, so smelting by hundreds of Indian hearth-place smelters, as was the practice, became inefficient. The underground ores required mercury, which came from Peru. Controlling the mercury meant controlling the mining companies. If you ran a company, you had to obey the rules to get the smelter to take your ore. If you ran a smelter, you had to obey the rules to get mercury. A half-dozen sophisticated smelters were set up using water power from 22 man-made lakes above the city.

The Indians laboured in the mines under horrid conditions. So many died that the Spanish had to import African slaves to replace them. The African slaves also died in vast numbers.

In 1572, Viceroy Francisco Toledo was sent from Lima to solve the problems proliferating across Upper Peru. He stayed four years. No ordinary administrator, he went to the heart of the troubles and his reforms determined Bolivian social life for centuries.

As the labour shortage became desperate, Viceroy Toledo expanded the ancient Incan taxation system called the *mitallos* or *mitas* and forced Indian men to work for the state one year out of every six, whereas the Inca had required only four months' labour every six years. Also, unlike the Inca, the Spanish paid nothing for the labour. The Indians worked 12 hours a day and stayed underground for four months at a time. Few men lived long enough to pay the full tax.

According to historians, over eight million men died from the start of the mining period until independence in 1825. If the figure is correct, 28,571 men a year—or 78 men a day—literally bit the dust.

Records show that even some Spanish found the conditions difficult. A priest saw the workers coming to town at the end of a working period, their eyes like those of ghosts, their backs scarred by the lash. "I don't want to see this portrait of hell," said the priest. "Then close your eyes," someone responded.

(See Chapter 16 for more about mining conditions in Bolivia today, and Chapter 9 for stories of the major mining barons.)

Psychological pressures from slavery were further illustrated in the last will and testament of a Spanish businessman. To show how the Spanish wasted money, he requested that one fourth of his silver be used to build a latrine in the city centre for nobles and plebeians both, as if nobles would consider using it next to an Indian. Another fourth was to be buried in his yard and protected by four fierce dogs that were fed using estate money. The third quarter was to prepare a feast for ditch worms to eat. The final quarter was for decking donkeys with jewels and gold vestments to accompany the man to his grave. His satire changed nothing.

Toledo didn't want a Spanish aristocracy to develop in Upper Peru but he allowed the Spanish to have estates, worked by tenant Indians, in the foothills from La Plata to Cochabamba and Tarija. This meant a secure supply of coca and food for the miners. When the Indians tried to leave the farms to live in larger towns, thus avoiding the life of serfdom, Toledo passed laws prohibiting this.

Minting

Toledo saw the obvious need for a local mint, so within his first year he hired the renowned builder Jerónimo de Leto, and the first mint in the Western world was constructed. It was used for 200 years before demand outgrew its size and a second mint was built, which is now a museum and major tourist attraction. Visitors without the nerve to go into the mines on Cerro Rico will get a taste of them from touring the mint that contains artifacts illustrating some of the hardships suffered by miners.

By the mid-18th century, Spain needed even more money to finance its wars in Europe. Silver production increased and the second mint mentioned above was built under the design of architect Salvador de Villa, who died four years before its completion. The chore was passed on to his pupil Luis Cabello, who then transferred the final responsibility on to Jaime San Just in

1765. Construction lasted from 1759 to 1773 and cost 1,148,452 pesos, which would be about 10 million dollars today.

Pressing machines were installed with a series of precision-made wooden gears and axles to mint ingots and coins. The source of power was simple: four mules, attached to a driveshaft, going round and round on the level below. By 1869 the mules were replaced with steam, and finally, in 1909, with electricity. The early coins were oddly shaped and made with 90 percent silver and 10 percent copper. Later coins were stamped perfectly round and contained 80 percent silver and 20 percent copper. Assurance of the quality was left to the assayer who, after inspection and approval, had to initial every coin minted. Production started with about 3,000 coins per day. Ironically, today Bolivia's two-boliviano coin is manufactured in Canada.

For shipping, the coins were put in safe chests with false keyholes and spring-loaded knives to slash the fingers of anyone trying to enter without the correct key. These locks needed to be opened in a specific sequence.

The 200-room mint of 1773, complete with courtyards and baroque decor, was a 15,000-square-metre (161,460-square-foot) building of carved stone, cedar wood, and brick. It was the largest building in South America at the time. Walls a metre thick were built to hold the heavy ceramic-tiled roof. The first courtyard contained the homes of the primary administrators, separated from each other by hallways. Outside each bedroom was a sign indicating the administrative position of its occupant.

In the main courtyard, near the entrance, is a fountain with a famous stone mask hanging above. Who the mask depicts is subject to great speculation. Some think it looks like Bacchus, the Roman god of wine. Others claim the mask is a cartoon of President Manuel Isidoro Belzu, who ruled

Potosí's icon at the entrance to the mint is believed by some to depict Bacchus, god of wine. Others believe it represents Spanish greed.

from 1848 to 1855. Still others think it could be one of the early directors because Eugenio Marin Moulon, the French artist who designed the piece in 1856, was known to dislike the director. Modern theories suggest the mask mocks Spain's greed. Today, the face has become the town's icon. Below the mask and facing the entrance is a still-in-use sundial called an equatorial clock. It has a bar parallel to the axis of the earth's rotation. Noon is indicated at the bottom of the disc, with 6 a.m. on the western side and 6 p.m. on the eastern side.

The Arch Cobija, used to separate the Indian section of Potosi from the Hidalgo or Spanish area.

Arches de Potosi

The Spanish liked monuments, and Potosi's wealth financed many, including those in the town itself. La Portada Torre de la Nave de la Compañion de Jesus, built between 1700 and 1707, is a Roman-style tower visible from anywhere in the city. Inspired by the design of the Arco de Triumfo in Rome, built in 315 AD, architect Sebastion de la Cruz added baroque touches and indigenous art for decoration. It is my understanding that La Portada had been built to honour the reign of Pope Leo X. On the day of independence over a century later, the tower's bells rang all day.

La Portada Torre de la Nave de la Compañion de Jesus, built between 1700 and 1707, is a copy of the Arch of Severus in Rome.

In the late 1980s, city council, unable to see the historical or cultural value of La Portada Torre, ordered it to be torn down. A huge struggle arose between city council and the citizens of Potosi. Finally a compromise was reached; the church behind the tower was destroyed and replaced with modern offices, but the tower itself remains intact.

The Arch Cobija, built of stone and mortar during Potosi's peak, was the border between the Indian sector and the upper city. The silver, loaded on donkeys, passed through the arch and down the valley, across the Altiplano to La Paz and finally down to the Pacific. Just beyond the arch, on the Indian side, is a wall held together with unique masonry made of powdered iron, chalk and egg white. The walls are so strong that today there is still no sign of disintegration. Now, the Arch Cobija separates the rich from the poor, which still mostly means dividing the whites from the Indians.

City Streets

Recently the centre of the city has been gussied up with pedestrian *pradas* lined with international restaurants and bars to impress the tourists. Around the edges old traditions prevail; there you'll see sidewalk merchants selling everything from *salteñas*, the Bolivian variation on the Cornish Pasty, to truck parts. Some of the streets tell their own stories: Hanged Man's Corner, Seven Corner Street, and Carbon Plaza, where rich Creole businessmen sold coal to poor Indians.

A few of the decorated doorways left over from Potosi's early days have overhanging balconies built in such a way that residents could clearly see if it was safe to enter the streets without encountering fighting gangs of soldiers and Creoles, or horse-drawn carriages plowing over anything in the way. Houses built on corners had two doors, one facing each street, to give occupants a clear view of both streets before leaving. All doors were painted green to keep out evil spirits. In 2002, city council decreed that the old houses, appearing much like they did 300 years ago, were to be painted in colours extracted from Cerro Rico.

Adding to the perils of the streets in the early days were at least 120 advertised prostitutes, housed in what were known as the best brothels on the American continent. There were also 36 gambling houses run by 800 professional gamblers, and 14 dance halls where alcohol flowed like Potosi silver.

Romeo and Juliet

Below the Arch Cobija in the Indian section is La Casa, a plain mud brick house with a cement balcony (recognizable by the "for sale" sign painted on the wall). According to legend, a beautiful woman fell in love with a young man of lower social status, and social protocol dictated that they should not marry. He often sang love songs to her from the street and she would stand on the balcony, hand to her agonized heart. Eventually the brothers of the woman killed the lover, and while his body lay in state in the church, she swallowed poison. The ghost of the woman searching for her lover is said to still haunt the house.

Looting by Water and Man

Potosi's story is mostly a sad one. In 1626 Lake Kari Kari, which was one of the 22 lakes that fed the smelters, broke its dam and flooded the city, killing thousands. So many in fact, that Spaniards, Creoles, mestizos and Indians were placed together in a common grave. The floods did not stop, so legend goes, until the priests paraded through the streets chanting and carrying a carved figure of Christ on the cross. Undoubtedly, rebuilding the dam also helped.

La Paz: an Outpost Becomes a City

The town of La Paz was originally a rest and recoup stop for the mule trains carrying silver from Potosi down to the Pacific. It was a wild and cold outpost along the Choqueyapu River that housed only travellers and military guards who entertained themselves by panning for gold.

It was the viceroy Pedro de la Gasca who decided to expand La Paz. In celebration of his 1548 victory over Gonzoles Pizarro, he ordered Captain Alonzo de Mendoza to build a new city in Upper Peru. Mendoza chose Laja, a spot on the Altiplano about 50 kilometres (30 miles) from present-day La Paz, and called it Nuestra Señora de la Paz. But Laja is barren and the winds are fierce. It took just three days for Mendoza to move to the mule-train outpost in the valley of the Choqueyapu River, where temperatures were warmer, winds calmer, water more abundant and soil rich enough to grow fresh vegetables. La Paz the city was born.

Presently, it is not a big city on the world scale, but is second only to Lhasa, Tibet, for the distinction of highest-altitude capital city. La Paz is built in a bowl through which the often-flooding Choqueyapu River runs, and it's the only city on the planet where real estate increases in value as the elevation drops. Besides the warmer climate and heavier air found at lower elevations, the pinnacles and spires of conglomerate rock and clay, sculpted by wind and water in the lower reaches of the bowl, make a dramatic backdrop for those living under them. Higher up the valley, the land becomes less stable and subject to frequent landslides during rainy season.

Within the first year of the city's inception, Juan Gutiérrez Paniagua became the community planner. His greatest achievement was designing the Plaza Murillo, which was then called La Plaza de Armas or, sometimes, Plaza de los Españas. Eventually the government buildings and cathedral were placed on the square, and the Indians were housed on the opposite side of the river, away from the centre. From the time of its completion to present-day, the plaza has witnessed frequent destruction and bloodshed. The worst times were during the great Aymara uprising of 1780, and again during the independence wars that began at the beginning of the 19th century. But even recently, as in the 2003 Tax War when the La Paz police took on the Bolivian army, the plaza was the scene of death and destruction.

4

COLONIAL RELIGION

Hierarchy

The Roman Catholic Church, then as now, has three basic organizational levels: Pope, bishop, and priest. At the very top of the hierarchy is the Pope, who is absolute, the world leader, the bishop of the diocese centred in Rome, and the priest of the Vatican parish. Under the Pope's command and at the second level are the bishops, who rule from a cathedral and run a diocese that includes many parishes, each with its church and priest. An archbishop is just a bishop with an especially big cathedral in an important city. A cardinal is a bishop or archbishop chosen by the Pope to sit on his advisory council. Each bishop is the priest of his cathedral. Under the bishops, at the third level, are the priests, each with a parish church. The bishops and priests have deacons as assistants.

Apart from the regular hierarchy are the monks and friars belonging to monasteries, and nuns belonging to convents. These groups attend to some of the church's practical activities like staffing hospitals, schools and orphanages. They also raise money by running businesses such as thrift shops, or collecting alms.

This bureaucracy came to Bolivia from Spain in the 15th century. The

Spaniards arrived looking for land and resources, but they brought Catholic clergymen with them who immediately built churches in the Indian villages, hoping to educate, "civilize" and convert. The diocese of La Plata was set up in 1552 under Bishop Thomas San Martin, who died seven years later and was replaced by Domingo Santo Thomas. This diocese incorporated most of what is now Bolivia. Half a century later, in 1605, the Dioceses of La Paz and Santa Cruz de la Sierra were established.

Catholicism would later become Bolivia's official state religion, written into the constitution. Article 2 from the 1880 version of the constitution read, "The State recognizes and supports the Roman Apostolic Catholic religion, the public exercise of any other worship being prohibited except in the colonies [Amazon, Santa Cruz, Chaco] where it is tolerated." Article 99 of the same constitution declared that "the government does not recognize divorce permitting remarriage and all disputes in marriage must be resolved through ecclesiastical tribunals," thus giving the church power to determine the outcome of civil problems. It would be almost 90 years before a constitutional amendment made a gesture toward religious tolerance of non-Catholics. (See Chapter 15.) Catholicism is still the dominant religion—and a huge cultural force—in Bolivia today, and has been throughout its history.

San Francisco Cathedral in La Paz

One of the biggest, boldest and most beautiful cathedrals in Bolivia is the San Francisco, established in La Paz by Father Francisco de Los Angeles in 1549 before La Paz was a diocese. The church's founding name is unknown, but it wasn't named after Father Francisco. That name came over 100 years later.

The original mud brick building crumbled under a heavy snowfall during the early 1600s. The rebuilding, using stone imported from the quarry in Viacha a few kilometres from La Paz, was started in 1743 and took ten years to complete, with most of the money coming from miners in the form of tithes and property taxes. Adventurous visitors occasionally stop in Viacha to explore the old town. The Andean-baroque design of San Francisco, common during this period, includes mythological creatures, mixed with local fruits, birds, animals (like the ever present puma), and flowers integrated into European architecture. Over the entrance is a carving of San Francisco Xavier, his welcoming arms outstretched. Inside, San Judas Tadeo, the patron saint of the poor and miserable, is visited often by the indigenous.

The church was finally named after Francis Solanus, a Franciscan monk who managed to recuperate, against all odds, from illness after working with plague victims in Spain. In appreciation for his blessing, Solanus sailed to America in 1589 to dedicate his life to the Indians. The ship hit ground just offshore from Lima during a storm. The lifeboats didn't have enough room for all the passengers, so the slaves, whom Francis was evangelizing, were left behind and Francis stayed with them. As the ship was ripped apart by the violent waves, he and the slaves salvaged pieces of wood and floated to a rock where they desperately clung for three days until help arrived.

Once ashore, Solanus learned to preach in the native languages and, in turn, was able to convert more Indians in less time than most priests. For these acts of "compassion and dedication," Pope Clement X canonized him in 1675. And once the new church in La Paz was completed, it was named after him.

Virgin of Copa and Francisco Tito Yupanqui

Copacabana held religious significance for the Indians due to its proximity to Lake Titicaca, but during the early days of colonial rule, the area attracted few Spanish residents because it was too far from civilized society and there was no gold or silver. The first Jesuit priests arrived in 1530 and had built a place of worship by 1552. The locals converted to Catholicism under the guidance of the Jesuits, but integrated some of their Indian customs into the rituals.

Francisco Tito Yupanqui, an artist and direct descendent of Inca royalty, was a practising Catholic living in Copacabana when the first version of the church was completed. One night, the Virgin Mary, dressed in elegant robes and carrying a child, came to him in a dream. He made a clay model of her likeness and placed it on the church's altar to honour her, but the religious authorities destroyed it, claiming it was of poor quality. Yupanqui made other reproductions but they, too, were rejected. Believing in his dream, Yupanqui studied at a reputable art school in Potosi. After years of learning he carved a wooden Virgin and took it to La Paz, where the church leaders again rejected his art. To emphasize their disgust, they kicked the carving down the stairs, smashing it to pieces. But Yupanqui salvaged the wood and, with the help of a priest from La Paz, restored the figure.

Yupanqui then took the Virgin to San Pedro de Taquina on Lake Titicaca, where town leaders placed her in their church under rigid protection. Don Geronimo Marañon, a powerful lawyer from Achicachi, saw the Virgin and insisted she become the patron of Copacabana.

Struggles over the possession of the Virgin continued until finally, on February 2, 1583, the image of the Dark Virgin of Candelária (as she became known) was smuggled back into Copacabana and placed on the altar.

Authorities might have booted her again but, shortly after her arrival, the Virgin was said to have started performing miracles. The first occurred when a gambler lost all his money except for a precious ring. He asked the Virgin for help, and sure enough he was soon rid of his gambling addiction. In appreciation, he gave her his ring and watched, mesmerized, as she spread her porcelain fingers so the ring could be slipped on.

The next miracle occurred in 1616 when Alonso de Escoto, a poor immigrant from Spain, wanted to make his fortune. He prayed to the Virgin

View from Horca del Inca, or the "pagan" hill, overlooking Copacabana, Lake Titicaca and the "Christian" hill.

for help, and then walked off with her earrings and two silver chandeliers, which he subsequently sold in Arequipa, Peru. With money in hand, he tried to purchase a winery, but the volcano nearby had rumbled, causing all the local wine to sour. Nevertheless, one proprietor talked Escoto into selling the wine-vinegar in Lima. When the casks were uncovered after their long journey to the port city, the liquid had mysteriously changed from vinegar into high-quality wine. Escoto sold it for a huge profit and, becoming repentant, returned to the church in Copacabana with a 300-kilo (650-pound) silver chandelier containing 365 lights. He placed it in the central nave.

Made of maguey wood, the dark-faced Virgin stands 84 centimetres (33 inches) high and has porcelain hands, arms and face. Her left arm cradles a gold cane and an indigenous boy-child, and her right hand holds a golden candle. Both the child and the Virgin have gold and silver crowns decorated with precious stones. The halo around the Virgin's head contains the sun, moon and 12 stars and she is adorned with a necklace, bracelets, rings and earrings, all heavily decked with semi-precious and precious stones. Her belt, a gift from Augustinian monks, has a two-inch ruby positioned in the leather. Embedded in her foot is a miniature Bolivian flag.

After the Virgin became known for performing miracles, priests felt that the mud brick cathedral in which she resided needed improvements. Though there is some disagreement on the date, they began replacing the mud brick as early as 1589 and completed the work as late as 1820. The present white-plaster-over-brick building features Moorish-styled tiles on the domes and hand-carved wooden doors. There are no traces of the original building.

In 1925 the Virgin was crowned the Bolivian Queen and Copacabana

A decorated car is waiting for the priest's blessing. No one in Bolivia would drive a new vehicle without the blessing in Copacabana.

became the most important pilgrimage site in the country. Each February 2–4, the Virgin's identity is redefined with celebrations of music, dancing and bullfighting. During *Semana Santa* (just before Easter), thousands of pilgrims walk from La Paz to Copacabana hoping for another miracle.

On the west side of the cathedral, inside the Candelária, is a dark, stonewalled room where pilgrims ask for specific miracles. The walls are covered in wax images of desired items or painted signs with words like "to walk," "money," "Volvo," and "food." Outside, tiny reproductions of the objects of desire such as children, houses, llamas and so on can be purchased to donate to the Virgin and help speed the blessings along. This church is also famous for blessing both new vehicles and older cars embarking on long trips. The cars are decorated with streamers and flowers, blessed by the priest, and showered with confetti and *chicha*. No Bolivian in his right mind would drive a vehicle any great distance without going through this ritual. And, at a one-time investment of 50 *bolivianos* (less than US$7), it's cheaper than insurance.

Churches of Potosi

Bolívar's revolution, during the early part of the 19th century, saw the contending armies of Royalists and Republicans sack the city many times, carting off its wealth. General Sucre, second president of Bolivia, instituted anti-clerical reforms in 1826 that stripped the church of its political power, although individual churches continued to amass great wealth. Only with 20th century tourism has there been some attempt to restore the glory of Potosi's churches.

There were 86 churches built in Potosi at its height, and 34 of them still stand, displaying architecture that is a sampling of the artistic richness of the time. San Lorenzo is the finest example in Bolivia of Andean-baroque art. On the other hand, the Church of Bethlehem, completed in 1753, was such a practical building it was transformed from a church to a hospital, and then to the Faculty of Arts and Sciences for the University of Potosi, and finally to a public theatre. Twenty-five of the 34 churches still standing were originally built for Indians.

San Martin Cathedral, constructed of mud brick in 1559, was the most prominent church built specifically for the Indians. It was originally made of mud brick, and then later was reinforced with stone and redesigned in the Andean-baroque style. One interior mud brick wall was retained as a reminder of the church's humble beginnings. The Andean-baroque form that combines European baroque with Indian designs was popular in the 16th century and was probably meant to entice the Indians to worship, particularly since the Indians were included in developing the style. Even so, many buildings throughout Spain and Latin America, including this one, have two door knockers, one set higher to be used by those on horseback (certainly not Indians) and one lower for those on foot.

The elaborate convent of Santa Teresa, built in 1685 by the Order of the Carmelites (notice the coat of arms over the door), is an example of the harsh treatment directed at some Spanish women.

A prospective nun accepted at Santa Teresa would pass through the heavy wooden doors at the young age of 15. Once the doors clanged shut, the girls never saw nor touched their families again. They were allowed one visitor a month for one hour, during which time they sat behind a screen and whispered. The rest of their confinement was spent embroidering, thinking of and praying to God, and speaking to the other 20 members of their sect for no more than two hours a day.

The nunnery never had more than 21 women in residence, and only when one died was she replaced. The girls who entered were the second daughters of aristocrats with dowries worth 2,000 pieces of gold, plus an exquisite dress that was worn by the girl at the time of entry. The gown had to be embroidered with gold thread and pearls or precious stones and was given to the mother superior, who did God knows what with it. Some of these gowns are now on display at the convent's museum.

For excitement, the nuns practised flagellation—some used barbed iron whips. Visitors can still peer into the glass-topped coffin to see the surprisingly intact body of Santa Maria de José de Jesus, a Paraguayan nun and the convent's founder, wearing a habit rather than a donated gown. (Frankly, I imagined some wild scenarios caused by the sexual repression of 21 women—picture nuns dancing over a non-embalmed body lying in a coffin encased in the church floor.)

Sucre Cathedral

Sucre, like Potosi, has a huge array of religious buildings. The cathedral, probably the richest in Bolivia, was started in 1551 and took 15 years to complete. However, to hold the city's many treasures—of which the Virgin of Guadalupe is one—sections were added for the next hundred years. Sitting over the central altar, the Virgin is bedecked in a robe of pearls, diamonds, rubies, emeralds and gold and is worth many millions of dollars. Among other treasures still on display in the church's museum is a diamond that Bolivians claim is worth more than the Hope, a 45.5-carat gem that twinkles from a case in the Smithsonian Natural History Museum. Some sources value the Hope at a quarter of a billion dollars, while more conservative assessors suggest US $200,000. A practical estimate is whatever some billionaire is willing to pay.

A copy of the Virgin of Copacabana sits above the carved doorway of the Cathedral.

The priests' gowns, also on display in Sucre, were designed to match the rest of the cathedral. They were adorned with gems and pearls and heavily embroidered with gold and silver threads.

Santa Cruz de la Sierra Missions

These missions, recently restored to their full splendor, are, in my opinion, far more impressive than any cathedral you will see in Bolivia. Watching *The Mission*, a film with Robert de Niro, will give you a very rough idea of what they are like, and of the history behind them. A short train ride out of Santa

Cruz will put you on the mission circuit, visiting some of the most functional and unique churches in the world.

While the rest of America's Indians were suffering slavery, starvation and disease, those living in the dry lowlands of the isolated Chaco, the semi-nomadic Chiquitano and Guarani Indians, were prospering. Although the Jesuits worked hard, they had little success attracting the Chiquitanos before 1691, when Father José Francisco de Arce arrived in the wake of a smallpox epidemic. He was looking for a shortcut to Asunciòn, the provincial capital of Paraguay and the Jesuit headquarters for the Guarani Indians. Seeing the need for medical attention at the village in present-day San Javier, he delayed his journey and developed a *reduccion*, a self-sufficient, socialist-styled community that included a good hospital.

The success at San Javier encouraged other Jesuits to move to the next settlement and then on to the next, building hospitals and missions as they went. Although they were often killed by hostile tribes, or died travelling through the swamps of the Pantanal, they persevered. The extreme isolation prevented authoritarian scrutiny, so the Jesuits were able to bend some of the church's rigid rules. The priests learned local languages and helped

San Ignacio de Loyola Mission, designed by Martin Schmid and Father Juan Mesner, was dedicated mostly to the arts.

prevent the spread of diseases by building communities in difficult-to-reach and isolated areas. Fatalities due to the smallpox epidemic were 11 percent in the Bolivian mission area, whereas the rest of the country suffered much more severely at anywhere from 35 percent to 80 percent loss.

The *reducciones* gave the Indians a peaceful, safe environment and a sustainable economy. The priests built schools, hospitals, prisons—and trust. They developed dictionaries and taught the Indians to read in their own language. They integrated Indian religious practices into Catholic rituals rather than insisting on rigid old-school services. Residents of the *reducciones* elected mayors and town councils who governed. No money was exchanged between members of each *reduccion*, though money was used for outside commerce. All food was shared equally. They even allowed those not wanting to convert to Catholicism to live in the towns and partake in all the social benefits.

Being moneylenders and economic wizards, the Jesuits financed the Indians to cultivate farms and make saleable crafts from grass, wood and leather. They taught them mathematics and the Indians, with the Jesuits as overseers, sold the produce and products at reasonable prices, thus giving the Indians equal status in Spanish commerce. This was something never practised with other native cultures in all of America. The Jesuits were so successful that some *reducciones* grew to over 20,000 inhabitants—a huge number, considering Buenos Aires had a population of about 25,000 at the time.

Later, the Jesuits used music to entice the Indians into religion. Father Martin Schmid, a musician from Switzerland, was a man with tremendous energy and imagination who came to the Chaco in 1729 to an already established *reduccion*. When he arrived there were numerous *reducciones* and five missions in the surrounding area, all prosperous.

Father Schmid was obsessed with music, especially the baroque styles of Bach and Vivaldi. He introduced to the mission churches a new architectural design with high ceilings and huge, open mud-brick halls covered in plaster and then ornately painted. The barn-like roofs were supported by carved tree trunks and had wide eaves to protect the walls from heavy rains. The architectural style offered excellent acoustics as well as relief from the overwhelming heat.

With boundless enthusiasm, Schmid directed choirs, handcrafted musical instruments such as flutes and violins, and copied thousands of pages of sheet music. He also taught the locals to sing, to make and play instruments, and to read the music he had copied. This encouraged them to settle in villages, which gave the Jesuits an opportunity to persuade the Indians to give up things the church disapproved of such as their nomadic lifestyle, infanticide and polygamy.

In exchange, the Indians laboured by building the missions, which was a long and arduous job. The mission at San Miguel, for example, took 200 men working every day for 11 years to complete. According to anthropologist Sofia Savedra Bruno, the Jesuits tried to combine traditional Chiquitano architecture with European techniques. Mission towns were built in the shape of a cross, with the plaza in the centre. This represented the nave of the church and was reminiscent of European designs. Traditional communal row houses, with short doorways and no windows, were placed along the arms of the cross. These cave-like dwellings kept out the oppressive heat of the Chaco.

One thing that bothered the Jesuits was that the birth rate in the Bolivian missions was lower than that of the Paraguayan missions. And the church wanted more souls, so the priests rang church bells an hour before sunrise to encourage sexual activity. This just shows how little the Jesuits knew about sexual activity! A census taken in 1706 at one mission showed that only 43 percent of the population was female, potentially causing a partnering imbalance. The low female population has recently been attributed to the high death rate of female children due to lack of nutritious food or medical care. Boys were given preferential treatment, especially during times of hardship because they could hunt and do the heavier farm jobs contributing to crop success. Many women also died in childbirth. To counteract the low birth rate, it's perhaps reasonable to assume that sexual activity had to be encouraged.

As the independent mission towns accumulated wealth, religious politics—often inspired by jealousy—became dangerous. In response, the priests trained the Indians in military techniques that helped them run off slave traders and unsavory settlers. To stave off a few problems, King Filipe II gave the Jesuits permission to deny any trouble-causing white man entry to the *reducciones*. This excluded officials like the governor, but the practice of isolation caused disgruntlement among other religious orders. It was obvious that this idyllic relationship couldn't continue.

The Treaty of Madrid, signed in 1750 between Spain and Portugal, decreed territorial exchange in the Santa Cruz/Paraguay area. The exchange included seven *reducciones*, and when the Portuguese moved into the camps, they encountered resistance from the Guarani, who were the legal owners. War broke out between 1754 and 1755 with the Jesuits supporting the trained Indian military. Their most active enemy was Bernardo Ibanez, a former priest who had been removed from the Jesuit order in Paraguay. He testified against the Spanish Jesuits and inspired resentment from across the sea. Ibanez claimed the Jesuits hoarded wealth and gold treasures and evaded taxes. He also reported the Jesuits as being haughty yet intriguing. In retaliation, the Catholic kings in Europe banned the Jesuits from all lands belonging to Portugal, Spain and France. Finally, Pope Clement XIV closed the order completely. King Carlos III of Spain had no choice but to expel the Jesuits from Bolivia. When the soldiers came, the priests went without resistance, while the Indians melted into the jungles. The 29 *reducciones* and 11 missions were left to fall into disrepair. By 1767 the missions had all been looted, often by church officials.

Two hundred years later, restoration of the missions started under the leadership of architect and priest Hans Roth, with the help of Father Godofredo Trenker. Roth was inspired after finding 5,000 pieces of handwritten music decaying under rubble in one of the abandoned missions. Some of the music pieces were by Zipoli Domenico, a European composer who lived from 1688 to 1726. It is now believed that Father Schmid must have brought this music with him from Switzerland, along with works by Vivaldi and Corelli. After Roth found the music, he spent the next and last 30 years of his life restoring the missions and reconnecting with the Indians.

5

MARCH TO INDEPENDENCE

Historians have concluded that the colonial period in Latin America ended for three reasons: Napoleon's conquest of Spain, constant Indian wars, and the European enlightenment that took place from about 1750 to 1800 and fostered revolutions in Europe and the Americas. In South America the struggle for independence involved a number of factions: supporters of Napoleonic Spain, supporters of the Spanish royal family who represented the old independent Spain, supporters of Bolívar (fighting for a Republican federation of South American states) and supporters of local strongmen who wanted the different Spanish viceroyalties to become independent countries under their control. The Indians were left to figure out which faction would best look after their interests.

Napoleon

The Bourbons had run France and Spain for a couple of centuries. Spain had a huge empire but France was more powerful, and family politics usually resulted in disadvantages to Spain. For example, the French kings were mainly interested in European power politics, not in Spain's vast overseas empire. When Louis XVI was beheaded in 1792, Spain joined Britain and Holland in "containing" the revolution. That failed, and Napoleon led the French to victory, taking over much of Europe—including Spain. The British continued fighting, acquired Portugal as an ally, and together they defeated the Spanish army now fighting for Napoleon. The French helped the Spanish invade Portugal to drive the British out, but the army and the people were demoralized by the struggle. Partisans joined the British to get rid of the French. By 1808, feuding within the Spanish royal family between King Ferdinand VI, the queen Maria Louisa of Parma and the queen's lover P.M. Godoy, who was a strong supporter of Napoleon, caused even more dissention in Spain. When King Ferdinand went to France to ask for support from Napoleon, he was told to abdicate, and he did. He was replaced by Napoleon's brother Joseph Bonaparte. The Spanish rebelled and the War of Independence began, resulting in the popular King Ferdinand VII ascending the throne. A long war against Napoleon, with British troops assisting rebellious parts of the Spanish army along with Spanish civilian resistance fighters, started. After Napoleon fell, Ferdinand eliminated liberal reforms that had taken place under French influence, and restored absolutism.

It's against this backdrop in Europe and in Spain that the independence wars of South America should be examined. In South America it was a five-sided battle and the alliances kept shifting, as is common with any political struggle. First there were the Indians, who wanted to be considered equal. They saw the growing struggle for power between their Spanish and Creole (those of Spanish blood born in America) overlords, and aligned themselves with whoever was more beneficial to them. Sometimes they fought for the sheer pleasure of wiping out a particular *patrón* and his family, or for the equal pleasure of just striking back at whites in general.

Second, there were the Spanish Loyalists who had been organized by Ferdinand VI to resist the British and Portuguese. They backed Spain, whether it was French-dominated (which meant more liberal) or not. After Ferdinand's death, his half-brother Charles III and his son Charles IV continued to support this resistance on both sides of the Atlantic. In 1776 the first Viceroyalty of Peru, which included parts of Chile, joined forces with the new Viceroyalty Rio de la Plata of Argentina to rule Bolivia, Paraguay, Uruguay and Argentina. The two viceroys were responsible for protecting their territory from Portuguese and British invasion. Under the leadership of Manuel Lobo, the Portuguese built a fort along the coast of Uruguay to prevent Spanish expansionism and to challenge the seaport monopoly in Lima, where all commerce in Spanish South America was routed. The South American Portuguese promoted the use of the deep-sea ports at Buenos Aires and Montevideo along the Atlantic.

The third group was the Royalists who fought Napoleonic Spain until 1815—the year Napoleon was defeated and Ferdinand VII took over again. In South America, a powerful second group of Royalists supported Carlota, King Ferdinand's sister, who governed Brazil with her husband Prince John of Portugal and who wanted a united front with her brother in Spain. After 1815, the Spanish group of Royalists, with their desired leader on the throne and the French defeated, had what they wanted: a royal leader. The Royalists in South America joined forces with the group in Spain and together they undertook to rule South America under the leadership of Carlota, her husband and Ferdinand.

Fourth were the Republicans (Bolívar and San Martin) who wanted independence and democracy for Creoles. They were inspired by the American Revolution and by the writings of Tom Paine, John Locke and Jean-Jacques Rousseau. Their cause was complicated by arguments over whether to form a federation or to keep each of the Spanish colonies as separate democratic states. Their revolution started in 1806 in Venezuela, and in 1812 in Argentina.

Fifth, there were the ambitious warlords who fought the Spanish, sometimes siding with the Republicans, and sometimes with Carlota and Prince John of Brazil. Because the land was vast and difficult to protect, the warlords often exercised authority using their own laws, unchallenged. One example is Pedro Antonio Olañeta in Upper Peru. He saw the Spanish defeated by Bolívar and San Martin, but refused to set up a Republican government. So Bolívar sent Sucre to kick Olañeta out, which he did. In the long run, though, warlords like Olañeta finally won: Bolívar's Republican governments—set up in Bolivia, Peru, Ecuador, Colombia and Venezuela—were continually at odds with Bolívar's federation. These Republicans wanted independence from Spain and independent states in South America. They regularly turned to their generals to take control or were simply taken over.

Newmarket Public Library (NPL)

Self Circulation Receipt

Date: 8/23/2016 Time: 11:18:39 AM

Name: HOMER, DAVID H.

Fines/Fees Owed: $0.00

Items checked out this session: 2

Title: Understanding Bolivia : a traveller's history
Barcode: 35923002510438
Due Date: 09/13/2016 23:59:59

Title: A concise history of Bolivia
Barcode: 35923003028778
Due Date: 09/13/2016 23:59:59

Phone 905-953-5110
Visit us on the web @ www.newmarketpl.ca

Thank you!

Newmarket Public Library (NPL)

Self Circulation Receipt

Date 8/23/2016 Time 11:18:39 AM

Name HOMER, DAVID H

Fines/Fees Owed $0.00

Items checked out this session: 2

Title: Understanding Bolivia : a traveller's history
Barcode 35323002510438
Due Date 09/13/2016 23:59:59

Title: A concise history of Bolivia
Barcode 35323003028778
Due Date 09/13/2016 23:59:59

Thank you!

Bolívar's vision was a united front—a federation of states that would make South America as powerful—if not more—as the US. For a good read, another description of these events is included in Gabriel García Márquez's novel, *The General in His Labyrinth*.

Túpac Amaru Rebellion of 1780

Some historians claim that Indian rebellions had no effect on independence. They may mean to say there was no direct effect. But the fact is, these rebellions represented a steady resistance that leaders like Bolívar cashed in on to recruit troops. He did this nervously and for good reason. Plenty of Indians enjoyed killing racist whites in retaliation for the oppression they experienced; even after independence, the Indians kept on fighting and still do today. But their contribution to independence as foot soldiers and allied forces is undeniable. Some of the more famous Indian insurrection leaders are Túpac Amaru I, Túpac Amaru II, Túpac Catari and Tomas Catari.

José Gabriel Condorcanqui, born in 1742, was a descendant of the Inca King and rebel Túpac Amaru I, who had been killed in 1572 in Cusco. Condorcanqui was an educated Spanish-speaking Indian who was embittered over the harsh treatment of the Indians. He changed his name to Túpac Amaru II, after his hero, and joined Indian groups to demand reforms in the mines and the textile mills and to campaign for improved housing, working conditions and pay scales.

In 1780, Túpac Amaru II and a few of his followers murdered the governor and *corregidor* (an official appointed by the king to control the peasant population) Antonio de Arriaga, who was known for his cruel tax collecting style.

The killing turned into a huge revolt with 60,000 Indians joining forces. Indian demands accelerated to include an autonomous region. Túpac Amaru II was captured in May 1781 along with his wife, his son Hipolito, his brother-in-law, his uncle and a number of military captains. They were all sentenced to death. In support of Túpac Amaru II's uprising, another Indian chief, Tomas Catari, led a rebel army into Potosi. He, too, was captured and hung. The head of Túpac Amaru II can be seen on old Peruvian 500 *inti* bills, printed until 1985 but since discontinued. (Modern Peruvian currency is the *sole*. Old *intis* can be found in second-hand shops along the Prada in La Paz.)

Two years later, in 1783, an Aymara Indian named Túpac Catari—the most notorious rebel of all—took up the cause. Born Julian Apasa, he was orphaned at a young age and raised by Catholic officials. Because he had never learned to read, as an adult he worked for subsistence wages as a common labourer and trader. But he was charismatic and knew that his people needed leadership. With the help of his wife, Micaela Bastidas, Catari gained the confidence of his people. He renamed himself Túpac Catari after his fighting heroes, Túpac Amaru and Tomas Catari, and led 40,000 Indian men into La Paz. They held the city under siege for 109 days, during which time Catari's army burned and destroyed many of the government buildings, including those on the Plaza Murillo. Over 10,000 residents—a third of the permanent population—died of starvation and disease before the siege ended.

In retaliation, the Spaniards sent in an army strong enough to force the Aymara to retreat. However, within a short time, they regrouped and dammed the river above the city. When the dam broke, it caused some damage, but not enough to cripple the town or the townspeople.

The siege resulted in the Spanish executing thousands of Indians and publicly quartering Túpac Catari. The Spanish also captured his 12-year-old son, Fernando, and sent him to prison in Spain for life. A superficial peace lay over the country, but the desire for self-government and independence was always beneath the surface. The Creoles wanted out from under the Spanish, and the Indians wanted out from under the Creoles and Spanish.

Túpac Catari's legendary status was not resurrected until the 1960s, when a group of Aymara peasants amalgamated the peasant unions into the Túpac Catari Movement. A massacre of protesting Indians in Cochabamba in 1974 led to the movement spreading to La Paz. It gained popularity and united peasant unions throughout the country. They eventually formed the Centro Obrera Boliviana (COB), a strong political labour organization still active today.

Pedro Domingo Murillo

Pedro Domingo Murillo was born in La Paz in 1757 to a priest and his Indian wife in a house on Calle Jaén. The street is famous for its cluster of museums, and his home, now also a museum, is popular. During his early years Murillo studied law in Cusco, but his relatively low social status (born to a Creole father and an Indian mother) led him to leave school before graduation and go to work in the mines near La Paz. He entered the army during the Indian rebellions between 1780 and 1783 and was rapidly promoted to the position of General Rosebuin's aide. But Murillo didn't want to back Spanish authority, so he resigned and worked as a merchant in a paper shop. This enabled him to print scathing broadsides conceived during meetings at the house on Calle Jaén, where he and his friends spent many nights working toward revolution. They envisioned a rebellion that would lead to independence from Spain for Bolivia, and autonomy from the Audencia of Chiquisaca for La Paz. Murillo was a Republican.

In 1805 Murillo joined an independence uprising in Upper Peru, but many of the rebels were captured and banished from the country. Murillo was thrown in prison.

His most famous follower was Father Medina, a radical priest who, with Murillo, wrote and distributed a famous paper that stated, "It is time to overthrow the yoke of the Spanish and organize a new government based on the interest of our fatherland ... Time to declare the principle of liberty in these miserable colonies acquired without any title and kept by tyranny and injustice."

Murillo and his followers also won the support of Mariano Michel, a freethinking radical and charismatic orator from the university of San Francisco Xavier in Sucre. Michel was good at stirring up discontent in the general population.

The rebels chose July 16, 1809, as their take-over date. It was the fiesta of the Virgin of Carmen, the patron saint of La Paz. The Virgin's statue was carried through the streets and the Indians played mournful tunes on their pan flutes as flower petals and confetti rained from the balconies. The revolutionaries mingled in the crowds until early evening, when they reconvened and attacked the army barracks, disarming the soldiers and ransacking the armament. They took the governor and bishop prisoners and called a town meeting, where they encouraged the people to ignore taxes on food, to burn town records of past debts and to "defend with their blood [the idea of] independence."

The city council, loyal to the separatists, made Murillo president because he claimed to be the enemy of Napoleon and an ally of Ferdinand, the rightful king of Spain. In fact, he was legitimizing the idea of independence by proclaiming La Paz an independent state.

A born leader, Murillo worked well with the Creoles, mestizos and Indians and tried to unite the Royalists and Republicans. Just one month after Murillo was made president of their newly formed Junta Truitiva, he led another revolt. By November Cochabamba, Oruro, Sucre and Potosi had joined the rebellion but they were a long way from La Paz. While the four cities were gaining momentum, an army from Cusco, led by Peruvian President Goyaneche and under orders from Spain, marched toward La Paz to end the mutiny. Many of Murillo's supporters, especially those in his new government, deserted him.

Plaza Murillo, also called Palacio Quemado (Burnt Palace) because of the many fires the buildings have endured.

Intrigue and betrayal continued until October 25, 1809, when the army from Cusco took control of La Paz. Murillo tried to negotiate a peace settlement but was arrested. Goyaneche then lured other revolutionaries to Murillo's house, where he arrested and jailed the whole lot. Court was held and Murillo, along with nine of his compatriots, became known as the Proto-Martyrs. They were lynched in the main plaza in front of the cathedral early in the morning on January 19, 1810. Thousands looked on as the noose was slipped around Murillo's neck. In a final act of defiance, he shrugged off the cloak he was wearing and yelled to the throng, "No one will be able to extinguish the torch which I have lit!"

Father Medina, Murillo's strongest adviser, was also condemned to death, along with 86 other rebels. Medina was able to escape to Chile to continue his activities, but all of the rest were executed.

Standing in the plaza today, one can't help but wonder from which ornate lamppost Murillo hung. His life was a small deposit in the payment of a huge bill that got Bolivians their constitution, part of which is inscribed on a stone tablet on the plaza.

Mothers of Cochabamba

Murillo's death only added passion to the desire for independence and more rebellions erupted around the country. The people of Cochabamba took Murillo's example in La Paz seriously and claimed independence for their city as well. After General Goyeneche suppressed the rebels in La Paz and hung Murillo, he moved to the other cities to squelch their enthusiasms. On May 27, 1812, his army marched into Cochabamba and killed hundreds. With most of the men dead, the women and children, led by the nearly blind,

Monument to the Mothers of Cochabamba who joined forces and helped defend the town against the Spanish.

60-year-old Joséfa Manuela Gandarillas, joined arms and helped defend the town. Although most of the women were massacred, they successfully held off the Royalist army for a number of hours. Today, a statue commemorating their heroism overlooks the city from San Sebastian Hill, and Mother's Day is celebrated on May 27 throughout the country.

Bolívar

The fight for independence in South America began at two ends of the continent, with José San Martin's rebels in Argentina and Simón Bolívar in Venezuela. According to author Egon Larsen, the story of Bolívar as a serious liberator started late in the afternoon of July 5, 1811.

Under a blazing hot Caracas sky, thunder boomed, the ground shook violently, and the quaking earth opened to swallow 10,000 people. Buildings crumbled, churches collapsed and thousands scrambled to free those still alive under the rubble. One man, eyes burning from the dust, stumbled from the home he'd lived in all his life and started wandering the streets. He came to the Chapel of San Jacinto and started to dig.

"You're to blame for God's curse," a second man yelled at him. "It's you and your rebels who have caused nature to strike us, because you have betrayed our king appointed by Him."

"You fool," answered the man. "Go and tell your friends that we are free, Venezuela is free and if nature is against us, we shall fight nature until all of South America is free."

The first man then went to the town square, where a monk was preaching on the sins of the people for betraying Spain. "Long live King Ferdinand," cried the monk, and the crowd replied, "Long live Spain, King Ferdinand and the Holy Inquisition!" The monk saw the first man and pointed a craggy finger, accusing him of bringing down the Lord's wrath.

The man, in blind fury, grabbed his sword and struck the monk dead. "Guard!" he said. "Disperse these people, dig out the living from the rubble, and bury the dead. I am your commander, Simón Bolívar!"

Judging from the style of its telling, this story is probably in part a myth meant to convey three things that were basically true: first, that Bolívar had presence and determination; second, that the church didn't like rebellion;

Statue of Simón Bolívar. The Liberator lived from 1783 until 1830.

and third, that the people Bolívar liberated were religious Royalists/Loyalists who couldn't be counted on.

Bolívar was born Simón José Antonio de la Santisima Trinidad de Bolívar y Palacios (thankfully historians simplified his name!) of lower aristocracy in Caracas, Venezuela in 1783. He became, after a lifetime of attempts, the liberator of Creole South America.

Enticed by free land and Indian labour, Simón's ancestors came to South America from Spain, developed a comfortable estate and worked mostly as lawyers, administrators and priests. Simón's grandfather made it up the aristocratic ladder until he became Governor and Captain General of Venezuela, representing the King of Spain. Simón's father, on the other hand, was the first within his family to become disgruntled with Spain's exploitation of the colonies, and even more dissatisfied with the second-class treatment he and those of his class received as colonials.

After 250 years there was still no fair exchange between the old world and the new. Non-religious, Spanish-American schools for children did not exist; travel away from America was restricted except by special permission from the king; and the settlers had no power in administering the land in which they lived and worked. Import and export taxes impoverished those in commerce, and even seats at the theatre or bullfight were distributed according to place of birth, with first-generation immigrants from Spain having the best choice of seat. To this day when travelling in South America, you will be told that certain people are *"Castellan"*—meaning they are "upper class" Spaniards. (I was often told, *"Soy Castillano"* before any conversation proceeded. This established our class differences, with me of course being considered of lower status.) Besides being aware of unfair treatment, the Creoles also saw, to the north, the success of the US's break from Britain.

As a youth, Simón Bolívar was unaware of the popular political discussions. His father died when he was three and his mother a year later, thus leaving him and his brother in the care of an indulgent uncle and a house full of servants. Simón grew into an uncontrollable child: willful, short tempered and restless. Yet he had a charismatic smile that could win the sternest heart.

After a long line of unsuccessful tutors, Simón was teamed up with Simón Rodriguez, an eccentric intellectual who had roamed the world, often as a peasant but always with a copy of Rousseau's *Emile* in hand. In the book, Rousseau, through the character Emile, describes how to bring up a young man so that his intelligence and goodness is not perverted by the rules of a governing, dominant society. Emile is raised and educated naturally, breastfed, given lots of love, attention, freedom and time outdoors. He is introduced to learning only as his mind is mature enough to grasp the ideas. He grows up free and informed, ready to play his part as a citizen of a democracy.

So Rodriguez took his young protégé Simón mountain climbing and exploring while talking about the French Revolution and the rights of men. After six years of companionship, Rodriguez was involved in an anti-Spanish plot and was banished from Venezuela, but his influence on Simón had already been strongly established.

With the departure of Rodriguez, Simón became a cadet in his father's regiment and studied tactics and strategy. He won consent from his uncle to continue his studies in Spain, where the people were not reacting well to

Napoleonic rule, although there was some support among the more liberal-minded. Napoleon had been made First Consul in France, where he began his dictatorial rule. He introduced law codes and taxation systems that spread with his conquest.

In Spain, Simón changed from an uninformed provincial to a well-heeled and educated Castellan, learning military procedures and hob-knobbing with the aristocracy. But he noted Spanish society was rife with corruption and degradation, spiced with cruelty and injustice. He threw himself into his military studies with even more ferocity, intending to use his learning not to rise with Napoleon's Spanish army but to one day fight for a republic of Venezuela or better still, a federation of South American states.

Simón met and married the love of his life while in Madrid, and went home to Venezuela to set up housekeeping. Shortly after arriving in Caracas, his wife became ill with fever and died. It was 1803 and Simón was just 20 years old. He was devastated. First he had lost his parents during his most impressionable years, and then his wife during his most passionate ones. Depressed, he returned to Spain, joined the idle rich and caroused until he was asked to leave by the government on pretext of food shortages.

He went to France and continued his fun. He was handsome and capti-vating, with dark curls, straight teeth and nose, and twinkling black eyes. He had no trouble getting access to high society. But a chance meeting at one social event with Alexander von Humboldt, a German scientist, renewed his sense of purpose. Humboldt talked about independence for South America, and the idea caught Bolívar's imagination.

Bolívar thought about his tutor Rodriguez and went to visit him in France. When they parted, Bolívar swore on bended knee: "I shall not rest until the shackles that bind us to Spain are broken and America is free..."

In 1810 Napoleon invaded Spain. By then Bolívar returned home with his compatriot Francisco Miranda, raised an army, and on April 10, 1810, he freed Venezuela.

The next 15 years of Bolívar's life oscillated between battles won and lost. But something happened to Bolívar's idealism over time. This was partly because of men like Santa Cruz and Olañeta: those like Santa Cruz followed Bolívar but had other ideas, and those like Olañeta opposed him as he opposed the Spanish. Some of the change came with age and wisdom. By the time Bolívar wrote up the Bolivian constitution in 1826, the changes in his thinking were obvious. He was much more conservative. He had come to two important realizations: that his fellow Creoles were not ready for democracy, and that the Indians would have to continue in serfdom.

Throughout his life Bolívar believed tyranny and anarchy were the two threats to democracy, but his constitution leaned heavily toward tyranny. It provided Bolivia with three legislative chambers divided into tribunes, senators and censors, a complicated administrative system, and a president for life. The senators were to oversee the laws and religious worship and were elected for eight years. The tribunes were responsible for finance and defence and held office for four years. The censors were responsible for upholding morals and recommended candidates for the Supreme Court and high administrative positions in the church.

This mixture of fascism and democracy couldn't work well. The mostly white property owners, who were only 10 percent of the population of about one million, elected the ruling officials, and Indians were disenfranchised because they were not considered official property owners. All local administration was appointed by the legislature, so offices became gifts from friends. A president for life who could appoint his successor meant that the ultimate leader was really a dictator. Bolívar also made the vice-president a hereditary position; power could fall into the hands of one family. The president was stronger than the legislature, and could therefore easily change the constitution.

Throughout his life, Bolívar wanted a united South America democratically ruled under the American model. What he produced was mostly—although by no means completely—a group of dictators that thought only of staying in power.

So a pattern for continual rebellion was set in South America. There have been 190 revolutions and coups in Bolivia alone so far. It is a history of constitution, revolution, new president, new constitution and revolution again, resulting in 80 presidents and 27 provisional presidents—an average of one every 15 months since the country's inauguration.

General Sebástian Francisco de Miranda y Rodriguez

Bolívar may have been the first to succeed at freeing South America, but he was not the first to try. General Miranda had raised a rebellion in Venezuela in 1806. He'd already led Spanish troops to help Americans win independence. He'd fought in the French Revolution, which resulted in his name being carved on the Arc de Triomphe. Thomas Jefferson, president of the US, facilitated his return to Venezuela in 1806. With a small army of 180 men and some British support, Miranda attacked the Spanish forces and lost miserably. He tried again and again, each time gaining little except the admiration of Creole youth. He met Bolívar in 1810, and joined forces under Bolívar's overall command. Together they liberated Venezuela. Miranda was made dictator on July 5, 1811.

The Spanish counterattacked. General Miranda, fearing defeat, singed an armistice in July 1812. Bolívar considered this treason. Bolívar, who then wanted Miranda shot, made the decision during a war council to turn Miranda over to the Spanish. When members of the war council woke Miranda at dawn and told him they were delivering him to the enemy, he remained composed and dignified. He held a lantern up to a council member and declared, "Noise! Noise! That is all these people can make!" Miranda made no other sound. After arriving at the Spanish Fort of San Carlos, he was charged as the instigator of the revolution and taken to the Four Towers Prison in Cadiz, Spain, where he died of natural causes on July 16, 1816.

Bolívar meanwhile established himself in New Granada (present-day Colombia). Because there was sympathy for independence, Napoleon's appointed viceroy in Colombia was expelled and an interim council installed. In 1813, while Miranda was rotting in a Spanish jail, Bolívar re-conquered Venezuela, lost it again and retreated to Colombia. The Spanish re-took Colombia too and Bolívar retired to Jamaica.

It was suggested Bolívar write a newspaper article about his fight for independence, which he did, although it was never published. The work, known today as "La Carta de Jamaica," was a summary of the revolution and an outline of how South America could reach independence and how the governments should be installed to run the new countries. It was an amazing vision.

José de San Martin

Born in Yapeyu, Argentina, on February 25, 1778, José de San Martin left for Spain at age six to study military strategy. As an adult he became an army commander. Like Bolívar, he found that Spain was still nominally independent, but really a subservient ally of France. The army was divided between loyalty to the King, who did exactly what the French told him to do, and loyalty to Spain. Rebel troops, resistance groups and an unhappy population were fighting back. The divided army had to put them down.

After one battle during the Napoleonic invasion of Spain, Martin watched a mob kill his commanding officer and then drag him through the streets. Martin forever after scorned the behaviour of commoners. But he chose to fight against Napoleon after Napoleon appointed his brother Joseph as King of Spain. Most of the country rose up, and San Martin was with them. He went on to fight in the Battle of Bailèn in 1808, when 23,000 French were trapped, without water, by 30,000 Spanish troops. Eventually the French agreed to surrender and San Martin was promoted to lieutenant colonel. The French retreated to the Ebo River and regrouped. The battles continued for five years, with the British navy and army supporting the Spanish. But what the Battle of Bailèn really revealed was that the French and Napoleon were not invincible and that they could be defeated. San Martin fought for two of the five years. Then, hearing about rebellions in Argentina in 1812, he left for Buenos Aires to help fight for independence there. By now he was a seasoned campaigner. In Argentina he formed the Regiment of Mounted Grenadiers, which became the best-trained militia in the independence movement.

The Battle of San Lorenzo, San Martin's first battle in America and his greatest win, resulted in his army of 150 men defeating about 250 Spanish Royalists who had more men and better weapons. Martin's army managed to kill 40 men and take 14 prisoners while losing only 26 men. During the battle, San Martin was pinned under his horse but a soldier pulled him out and sacrificed his own life to protect San Martin as he escaped. San Martin was then promoted from lieutenant colonel to general. By 1815, when Spain was finally free of French rule, the Spanish Royalists from Bolivia thought their time had come and invaded Argentina. San Martin defeated them as well.

After Argentina was freed, San Martin became an able governor, but Lima controlled neighbouring Bolivia as well as Chile. Bolívar controlled Colombia (New Granada) and was fighting in Venezuela. Both Bolívar and San Martin were aiming at Lima and Peru, the centre of Spanish power in America.

San Martin prepared his own invasion by spreading rumours throughout Spanish-controlled areas that independence supporters, numbering almost 3,000 men, were about to invade. He was attempting to instill fear and win local support. San Martin then headed across the Andes into Chile, intending to gain control there before moving up to Lima. Crossing the Andes was difficult with temperatures at +30°C (86°F) during the day and -10°C (14°F) at night, and with the 3,000-metre (10,000-foot) altitude to contend with. San Martin managed to free Chile after numerous battles—some easily won, others costing many lives. Once in Peru, San Martin occupied Lima and on July 28, 1821, he became "protector" of the independent nation. After a parliament was organized, he resigned and a year later, went to meet with Bolívar in New Granada.

"We shall meet and America shall never forget the day we embrace," San Martin said in a letter to Bolívar before departing for Guayaquil. There, San Martin hoped to receive support and advice from his long-time hero Bolívar for furthering the independence movement. But as they met, a letter came informing them of a revolt against San Martin by the Peruvian army. Distraught, San Martin said, "If this is true, I shall put an end to my public life." Bolívar hastened San Martin's departure by refusing to supply him with trained troops and arms to help regain control in Peru.

His pride diminished, his spirit beaten, San Martin returned to Buenos Aires, leaving most of his army under Bolívar's command. He settled business and moved to Europe, where he spent the rest of his life in quiet retirement. San Martin never knew that historians would include him with Bolívar as a major contributor in the freeing of South America, although he must have realized that he had left a stable government in Argentina.

Antonio José de Sucre

Antonio José de Sucre, Bolívar's top general and co-liberator of Bolivia, was born in 1795 in Cumanà, Venezuela, to a wealthy aristocratic family. His mother died when he was seven and he was sent to Caracas to live with his godfather, the archdeacon of the cathedral. Sucre graduated from the College of Military Engineers in 1810, after the independence movement was well under way, and he soon gravitated into the top ranks of the leaders.

His first promotion, in 1811, made him part of General Miranda's personal staff. After New Granada was liberated, the Spanish counterattacked in Venezuela. Miranda surrendered, Bolívar went into hiding in Jamaica and Sucre fled to Trinidad. In 1815 he went to Cartagena and helped that besieged city defend itself against the Spanish. The Spanish won and Sucre barely escaped by boat across the Caribbean. A storm wrecked his ship but Sucre clung to a tree trunk and, 20 hours later, was picked up half-dead from exposure and thirst. Meanwhile, Bolívar had attacked Venezuela with British and Haitian help, and had restored control. Sucre rejoined him, and Bolívar commanded Sucre to help annex Ecuador to Colombia.

Sucre was short and slender with a thoughtful expression. He was honest, kind, trusting, tactful, sincere and modest. The modesty became especially evident later when he was appointed to presidential positions but declined. He was promoted to colonel in 1817 and the Colombian general Francisco Antonia Zea made him brigadier general in 1819 when Sucre was just 24 years old. This promotion was unknown to Bolívar and, when Sucre was on the Oronoco River in Venezuela shortly after, he was approached by Bolívar's ship.

Bolívar called out, "Who goes there?"

Sucre answered, "General Sucre."

"There is no General Sucre," Bolívar replied.

"I would never consider a post without your consent," Sucre answered. Bolívar was silent for a moment and then said, "Come aboard, General Sucre." This act of humility by Sucre started a life-long friendship. He was given the honourable post of obtaining weapons, and in 1820, after the Battle of Boyacá , he was made Bolívar's chief of staff.

The Battle of Boyacá freed Venezuela permanently. Bolívar and Sucre left a Republican government in control and moved on to New Granada. They defeated the Spanish in Ecuador and united Venezuela, Ecuador and Colombia into the Republic of Colombia.

This was the first step in Bolívar's dream to unite South America into a place that could resist oppression from Europe and counterattacks from neighbouring countries. He also believed that, united, the provinces could work together without internal strife, but divided they would always be at war. Bolívar saw the emerging power of the US as an example of a federation formed from united colonies. What Bolívar couldn't see was that democracy, already practised in North America under the British by a people who were accustomed to parliaments and rule of law, was a foreign concept to the Creoles. The liberal movement in Spain had been completely crushed with the ejection of the French, and Spain went back to absolute monarchy.

Sucre was made president of the province of Ecuador but he preferred the thrills of battle to his administrative duties and joined Bolívar on his march to independence. While Bolívar and Sucre worked from the north, General José de San Martin defeated the Spanish in the south. He had crossed into Peru, negotiated a peace settlement and set up a new government. He was also called to a meeting with his hero, El Libertador, who was now in control of Ecuador. (See José de San Martin section above.)

Sucre and Bolívar fought at Junin in August 1824 and at Ayacucho in December, when they captured the last of the viceroys and liberated Upper Peru. With Peru free, the Spanish were pretty much finished. Sucre continued on to the Altiplano doing mop-up operations.

The Battle of Ayacucho is celebrated throughout South America in songs and poetry, and every year on December 9 with festivals. (*Aya* in Quechua means "soul" and *Kuchu* means "corner.") La Paz was renamed at the time as La Paz de Ayacucho; translated, this means "peace from Ayacucho." The most famous song, "*Adios Pueblo de Ayacucho*," commemorates the village of Ayacucho and is sung by Savia Andina, a Bolivian vocal group. Also sung by the same group is my favourite, "*Viva mi Patria Bolivia*," or "Long live my country Bolivia." Their music can be purchased in music shops in major centres of Bolivia.

Bolívar must have been relieved when Upper Peru was liberated, even though he harshly reprimanded Sucre for going to La Plata without being commanded to do so.

"You and the army are subordinate to me," Bolívar announced after Sucre declared La Plata free. "Your province is to carry out what I order. Neither you nor I, nor the Peruvian or Colombian parliaments, can break or violate the principles of law which we have recognized in America." After Sucre offered, in humility, to resign, Bolívar reneged and said, "A high destiny is in store for you."

When Sucre declared Upper Peru an independent state he did not consider the principle of *"Uti Possidetis,"* which was the basis of the independence movement. Uti Possidetis meant that each nation was to preserve the status quo of 1810, when Upper Peru was a province of Peru and a vice-kingdom of La Plata. In other words, he was supposed to treat Upper Peru as a province of Peru.

After the offer, Bolívar was once again satisfied with Sucre's loyalty and, after Bolivia's declaration of independence in 1825, he made Sucre president. Sucre in turn named Upper Peru "Bolivia."

In 1828 Sucre left public office and returned to Quito. There he fought an endless series of rear-guard battles and tried to squelch resistance to Bolívar. While in Ecuador, Sucre married the daughter of the Marquise of Solanda, Mariana Carcelen, and they had a daughter 10 months later. They made their home in Bogotá, Gran Colombia.

In April 1830, after the territory split and Colombia, Venezuela and Ecuador had become separate but established countries, Bolívar resigned with the intention of retiring in Europe.

On June 4, 1830, Sucre was riding home to Bogotá after a unification conference in Quito. Near the village of Pasto, he was shot in the head by the ambitious General José Maria Obrando, a supporter of Spanish rule who knew that unless Sucre lay dead, he would succeed Bolívar. Sucre's death was devastating to Bolívar.

In December of that same year, Bolívar died in the village of Santa Maria, Colombia, knowing that the united continent he had dedicated his life to obtaining was not to be. Terribly disheartened and ill from tuberculosis, he lay on his deathbed and declared, "He who makes a revolution ploughs the sea."

Pedro Antonio Olañeta

Bolívar had been stymied because not all citizens of South America wanted an independent and united country. There were Royalists like José Maria Obrando, still faithful to King Ferdinand, and there were those like Pedro Antonio Olañeta, who wanted to be top dog wherever they were. Olañeta was an example of the kind of people Bolívar and Sucre were contending with, and in many ways those people won out.

Olañeta was a Spaniard who immigrated to South America at age 17, made a substantial fortune as a merchant, and then entered the military. He supported King Ferdinand, but because he wanted to separate from Lower Peru, he refused to swear loyalty to Viceroy La Serna in Lima. Nor did he join Simón Bolívar and San Martin, battling for independence. The Viceroy of Lima sent 5,000 troops to change Olañeta's loyalty. For Bolívar fighting at Ayacucho, it was advantageous to have that many enemy troops busy elsewhere.

In La Plata, Olañeta filled parliament with loyal supporters, took command of his 4,000-man army, and proclaimed himself the Governor of the Provinces of Upper Peru. He was able to hold the Spanish troops at bay.

Once the Battle of Ayacucho in Peru was won in 1824, General Sucre, under command of Bolívar, entered Cusco and took the old Inca king's royal robes as a symbolic gesture of control. There were just two spots in South America not under the new Republic's control: the Port of Callao, the most important port on the Pacific situated 14 kilometres (9 miles) southwest of Lima, and Upper Peru, which was Olañeta's territory.

General Sucre thought taking these two places were just clean-up operations and asked for Bolívar's instructions. Those orders never came, so he headed out on his own toward Upper Peru while a few of his troops easily took Callao. In January of 1825, as General Sucre was marching toward La Plata, many of Olañeta's men, seeing the inevitable, abandoned him. By March all the present territory of Bolivia was under control of the new federation except for La Plata. Although Olañeta was given the choice of joining forces with the rest of South America, he refused. Sucre marched in on April 13, and in this final battle killed Olañeta and defeated his dwindling army.

Over the next five years, however, the South American federation fell apart. Men like Olañeta kept popping up, taking over local governments, declaring independence and appointing themselves president.

6

COLOURFUL PRESIDENTS

A few years ago the La Paz newspaper, *Ultima Hora*, took a poll to determine the seven most "historical" presidents of Bolivia. This was a good way of democratically determining something historians had not wanted to touch. In the first 50 years of Bolivia's existence, presidents were ousted frequently—some lasting three, four or five months and with one in power just five days. During the age of the *caudillos* (as the period from 1825 to 1865 is called), military strongmen, much like Pinochet in Chile, tried to run the country. Eighteen presidents came to power, six new constitutions were implemented and six presidential assassinations took place. Bolivia has had 107 presidents, including provisionals, since independence. Compare that with the 43 presidents the US has managed with since 1789.

Some of these Bolivian presidents are notable for being extremely efficient, or even good, while others are considered total nutcases.

General Mariscal Andrés Santa Cruz

Santa Cruz was one of the more competent presidents, even though some of his ambitions resembled Olañeta's. Santa Cruz was born in 1792 in La Paz to an Indian mother and a Spanish father. He studied at the Convent of San

Francisco and later at the San Antonio Abad Seminary in Cusco, although he did not graduate.

He joined the Spanish Army and fought against the independence fighters until he was captured near Tarija during the Battle of La Tablada in 1817. Today there is little to see at the battle site, but every April 15 and 16, a local festival marks the occasion and everyone, including foreigners, is welcome.

The independence fighters took Santa Cruz to Buenos Aires as a prisoner of war, but Santa Cruz escaped, went to Lima, and became the commander of the Chorrillos, a prestigious military company, to fight once more against the independence movement. He was again taken prisoner, only this time he was incarcerated at San Martín's headquarters, where San Martin soon convinced him to change his allegiances. Santa Cruz rose in the rebel ranks quickly. By 1822 he was brigade general of the Upper Peruvian troops (in present-day Bolivia). He joined Bolívar two years later and became his chief of staff. After the last battles for independence were fought at Junin and Ayacucho, Santa Cruz became the chief of staff in the Patriot Army and then marched into Upper Peru to be with Sucre, the Bolivian president. In April 1828 Sucre resigned, and four different presidents struggled for power. They governed in quick succession, lasting three months, four months, five days and five months. Santa Cruz believed he could stop these struggles, so he took over for 10 years, from 1829 to 1839. The Mariscal Andrés de Santa Cruz Library, located on the Plaza Estudiantes in the centre of La Paz, was founded in 1838 and named in his honour.

Although Santa Cruz approved a new democratic constitution, he quickly turned his own rule into a dictatorship. He cut the president's lifetime term to four years but gave the president the ability to dissolve congress. This made congress passive and submissive, effectively increasing the president's power even though his term was limited. Santa Cruz strengthened the army, purged conspirators, and introduced a Napoleonic civil and penal code that stressed a clearly written and accessible law.

He built the public treasury by instituting protective trade tariffs for the cotton industry, and he opened the port of Cobija on the Pacific, which was subsequently used for all Bolivian imports. By devaluing the silver currency, he was able to finance government activities and pay off foreign debt. He built roads, schools and two universities. Knowing that land was an important issue with the Indians, Santa Cruz tried to pass effective laws that would allow Indians to own property. He also set aside land for them to purchase.

In practice, many of these reforms did not work. Indians didn't make enough money to purchase land and those living on farms had to verify ownership in court by proving they had lived on their land for 10 years, a difficult task without expensive legal assistance. This caused such a backlog in court, with the Creole land-grabbers waiting impatiently in the wings, that Indians were declared illegal entities (similar to Indians being considered "non-people" long ago in Canada) and the courts were forbidden to recognize any claims they made. The indigenous population again became "wards of the state," and stayed that way until the 1952 revolution.

But overall, the strong 10-year reign brought relative stability to the country. And this stability allowed Santa Cruz time to pursue his greatest desire: to unify Peru with Bolivia and restore the Inca Empire, a gesture that acknowledged his native heritage.

He joined forces with Peruvian President Luis José de Orbegoso and suppressed rebels who were against unification. By 1836 the ambitious Santa Cruz deemed himself "Supreme Protector," which gave him enough authority to form the Bolivia-Peru Confederation, a confederacy recognized by the US, England and France but opposed by Chile and Argentina. Such a large confederation threatened Bolivia's two powerful neighbours, and they fought back. When Argentinean troops attacked, Santa Cruz was able to defeat them, but he did not succeed in a subsequent battle with Chile.

Santa Cruz resigned as "Supreme Protector" and was expelled from both Bolivia and Peru in February 1839. He fled to Ecuador where he plotted for his return to Bolivia politics. While he was busy planning, he was caught and imprisoned by the Chilean Army but later released. In 1846 Santa Cruz returned to Bolivia for an unsuccessful run at the presidency. After the election, President Manuel Belzu appointed him ambassador to several different European countries, but Santa Cruz still wanted to be the leader. He ran again, and lost once more. Disheartened, he retired to France and died in 1865.

One hundred years after his death, Santa Cruz's body was returned to Bolivia and honoured with a military burial. He was interred in a mausoleum in the cathedral on Plaza Murillo in La Paz, with his image reproduced in the stained glass windows over the altar.

Manuel Isidoro Belzu

Most noted for designing the Bolivian flag and for his idealistic but ineffective support of Indian rights, Manuel Isidoro Belzu was a military man born in La Paz in 1808 to poor parents of Syrian ancestry. This unfortunate station of birth denied him access to the aristocracy and influenced decisions he made during his presidency.

Belzu, dashing in uniform and charismatic in diction, rose rapidly through the ranks to become an officer in the army. Always ambitious, he conspired against the president, José Ballivián who, according to gossip, had seduced Belzu's wife, Argentinean poet Juana Manuela Gorriti.

An interesting aside: Juana Manuela was the daughter of a baker from Salta, Argentina. The family moved to Tarija where they opened a bakery and became known for their empanadas. Juana Manuela was nicknamed "Salteña," meaning the little girl from Salta, and the empanadas she sold eventually became known as *salteñas*. Today they are Bolivia's most popular snacks, available on every street corner for a pittance. Competition from the tasty and inexpensive *salteña* was one of the reasons McDonald's three outlets had to close shop in Bolivia in 2002.

Against the wishes of the aristocracy, but with the support of the lower classes, Belzu and the other generals succeeded in forcing Ballivián into exile. The government changed hands a few more times until December of the following year, 1848, when a successful coup gave Belzu the presidency for the next seven years, along with a de facto presidential seat for the following two.

Belzu appropriated some land and money for the Indians, who called him "Tata"—a colloquial and affectionate term for father. The appropriations were partly done to aggravate Ballivián, his wife's seducer; Ballivián's political practice was to impose heavy taxes on the Indians working on the Hildago-owned haciendas so that the Indians could not afford to leave and therefore could not establish farms on the lands that Santa Cruz had set aside for them. In practice, the laws Belzu introduced were ineffective and superficial and made almost no financial difference to the Indians. But some of Belzu's speeches on behalf of the peasantry are commendable.

During Belzu's reign, Bolivia's quinine production reached its highest levels. Through tariffs, quinine sales financed the military. Belzu needed the military to stave off his enemies, but that same military was also, on occasion, the source of opposition. During his seven-year dictatorship, Belzu faced 42 coup attempts—all led by military generals supporting either Ballivián or José Maria Linares, an aristocrat and skilled lawyer who in 1848 negotiated a treaty with Spain that recognized Bolivia's independence. In 1857 Linares led a coup that overthrew Belzu's administration.

Belzu's most notable contribution is the present-day appearance of the Bolivian flag. The design is based on a rainbow he saw while travelling from La Paz to Oruro: three horizontal stripes in red, yellow and green. Red represents blood spilt in the struggle for independence; yellow is for the minerals taken from Cerro Rico in Potosi; and green signifies the wealth of an agrarian society. Belzu also redesigned the coat of arms and placed the symbol in the centre of the flag's yellow strip. Bolivia's national flower, the Kantuta, was chosen years later because it shares the same colour combination as Belzu's flag. The chalice-shaped flower has a red cup with a yellow sepal that attaches to the green stem. (See Chapter 17 for the legend of the Kantuta flower.)

The coat of arms, also on the flag, has a llama in the centre. This llama, according to legend, saved a number of Indian lives during a battle for independence; the Indians were in a field, hiding behind their llamas as they waited for the attack, but the Spanish saw only llamas and left. Behind the llama on the coat of arms is an image of Cerro Rico, with the sun beaming down. Above the sun is a condor, the national bird, surrounded by a laurel branch and an olive tree. On the right of the condor is the red hat of freedom and on the left are guns and an Incan axe. The flag was raised for the first time at the Lighthouse of Conchupata in Oruro on November 6, 1851. The lighthouse is now considered a national monument, but is in such disrepair it looks more like a flophouse.

An attempted assassination of Belzu in Sucre by General Mariano Melgarejo's supporters convinced Belzu to flee to Europe, where he became the acting dignitary at the diplomatic mission. While there, he encouraged the Count of Aquila and the Bourbons in Naples to become monarchs of Bolivia. This was the solution, Belzu felt, to the country's complex problems. They declined.

He returned to Bolivia and sponsored his son-in-law, Jorge Cordova, as a presidential candidate. Through Belzu's political connections, Cordova won the presidency. Belzu then ruled through Cordova for the next two years.

A successful coup led by General Mariano Melgarejo in 1864 resulted in Cordova's removal from power. It was then that Belzu uttered his most famous words: "Bolivia is totally incapable of being governed." The words were repeated throughout the country for the next hundred years.

Belzu tried to regain power. He attempted to murder Melgarejo, but Melgarejo turned out to be stronger and killed Belzu by strangulation. The Bolivian people had believed that the corrupt Melgarejo was surely going to be overthrown, and a crowd had gathered in the Plaza Murillo waiting for Belzu to emerge victorious. They chanted for him to appear. But after Belzu's dead body was displayed from the balcony of the presidential palace, the people quickly changed their chant to, "Long live Melgarejo!" They knew instinctively that support for anyone but Melgarejo could cost them their lives.

General Mariano Melgarejo

Known among his enemies as the "scourge of God," Melgarejo earned his nickname from a number of violent performances enacted during his seven-year presidency from 1864 to 1871.

In addition to his reputation for viciousness, Melgarejo was a drunkard and womanizer who almost broke the public coffers to support his habits. He even went so far as to melt some of the church relics in Sucre to pay for his debauchery. His most famous words don't compare to Bolívar's anguish over the revolution, or Belzu's despair for the country. One of Melgarejo lasting legacies is the expression, "What best follows a cup of *chicha*? Another cup!"

As a military man, Melgarejo changed allegiances to suit his whims. Before becoming president, he led an unsuccessful coup against President Belzu. After the coup, Melgarejo was sentenced to death for treason but pleaded he could not be held responsible because he was drunk, and Belzu spared his life. After Linares became president in 1857, Melgarejo switched loyalties to General José Maria de Achà, who became president in 1861. Linares was immediately banned to Chile, where he died that same year. Melgarejo led a successful coup against Achà in December 1864.

Declaring himself the "most illustrious man of the year," Melgarejo forced his men into drunken orgies and, for entertainment, often made them roll around the palace floors like excited dogs. In this fashion, he raped and rampaged throughout La Paz. He was also known to debate with his soldiers the relative merits of generals Napoleon Bonaparte and Napoleon III. He preferred Napoleon III. During one drunken binge—determined to prove his point—he commanded his army to march overland (and overseas) to France to help Napoleon III with the Franco-Prussian war. The large body of water they needed to cross to get to France worried the soldiers until a sobering rainstorm in the Amazon made Melgarejo change his mind and march back toward La Paz.

Melgarejo is also credited with stripping naked the visiting British ambassador, tying him to the back of a mule, and sending him on his way because the ambassador's drinking abilities were not up to par with his own. The ambassador had also refused to kiss the behind of Melgarejo's mistress, ordered as punishment after Melgarejo had listened to the outspoken Brit's complaints. When Queen Victoria heard about this she ordered the British Navy to bombard La Paz with gunfire. After someone informed her that the city was, in fact, 200 miles inland, she declared that the country did not exist and would never again appear on British maps. One story has the queen cutting the country out of her map with a pair of scissors.

With a bit of a messianic streak Melgarejo was so bold as to declare Easter Sunday his birthday (April 13), forcing the churches to celebrate him as well as the resurrection on that day. What he did the following year, when Easter would not have fallen on his birthday, is unknown.

Melgarejo had delicate skin and often had sores on his face, which made shaving painful. Melgarejo advertised to pay a huge sum of money to any barber who could do the shaving without pain. After one young barber managed to succeed, Melgarejo asked how the barber could be so brave, knowing his life was in danger if he failed. "I hold the razor," the barber explained. Melgarejo rewarded the barber with the money and a high position in the military.

During one particularly decadent party, he traded 102,400 square kilometres (40,000 square miles) of prime land in the Amazon basin for a horse and the right to use the Amazon River as access to the Atlantic. But the government of Brazil was able to outsmart Melgarejo by blocking passage on the upper Madeira River between Bolivia and present-day Brazil, thus cutting Bolivia off from the Amazon.

Dealings with Chile, Bolivia's old enemy, fared no better. Melgarejo signed a treaty with Chile, dividing the Atacama Desert—once entirely owned by Bolivia—in half, with Bolivia keeping the mineral-rich north. In return Melgarejo received another horse and a large sum of money, which landed in his purse instead of in the national treasury. Acquiring the southern half of the Atacama gave Chile an appetite for the rest, and soon Chilean mining companies were exploiting the natural resources in the north. This provided the groundwork for the War of the Pacific, a major conflict that resulted in Bolivia becoming a landlocked country. (See "Hilarión Daza and War of the Pacific," page 93.)

Under the 1866 land decree, Melgarejo abolished the Indians' communal agricultural system on what was left of the Indians' territory, and forced them to pay a huge land tax. Not one Indian had the means to pay such an amount and, because of Santa Cruz's law of 1834, there was no legal recourse for them. Melgarejo seized their land and sold it at bargain prices to the wealthy white population who, in turn, allowed the Indians to work the land for them. When the Indians near Lake Titicaca rebelled, Melgarejo confiscated their land and sent his army to massacre them.

In 1871, Melgarejo's antics finally caused a coup led by General Agustin

Morales, one of the men who had helped put him into power. Melgarejo fled through hostile Indian villages on his way to Peru. Only five of his 300 soldiers survived the trip, but he managed to make it unscathed.

After Melgarejo left Bolivia, his mistress Juana Sanchez was imprisoned for unpaid debts she claimed weren't hers. Melgarejo heard of her plight and raised money in Lima for her release. She settled in Lima as well, but rejected Melgarejo. Distraught, he tried everything to renew their relationship until one night, a half-drunk and half-crazed Melgarejo tried to gain entry to her house. He was caught and shot dead by Juana's brother.

Some artifacts of Melgarejo's reign include a medal minted in Potosi in September 1865. On one side, the medal displays both his profile and that of Mariano Donato Muñoz, his civilian aide who was present at the signing of an allegiance treaty between Bolivia and Chile. On the other are the words *"Al Valor y Al Talento."* A second medal, with the words *"Porla Defensa. De La Constitucion En 20 de Diciembre de 1868 Potosi"* inscribed on one side and a portrait of Melgarejo on the other, was also minted. The medals sell on eBay for around US$30–$200.

There is also a bridge named after Melgarejo in Tarata, where he was born in 1820. The bridge once spanned a creek that has since dried up, so now it crosses a dusty depression in the middle of the street. His Tarata house is a tourist attraction, and documents bearing his signature can be seen in the Palacio Consistorial on the town plaza, along with other notable documents signed by Bolívar.

Historians have great fun with Melgarejo, mostly because he was such a colourful character. He embodies the Creole sense of inferiority that can only be hidden by an exaggerated display of masculinity. The term *"Melgarejoism,"* first coined in 1952 by Bolivian writer Gustavo Navarro (a.k.a. Tristan Merof), is used to describe a recurring theme in Bolivian politics. According to Navarro, this usage suggests that *Melgarejoism* is "the frame for Bolivian history: a feudal society that protects the military."

Hilarión Daza and War of the Pacific

Bolivia's first major modern war, the War of the Pacific, took place between 1879 and 1884. It was a turf war over the long strip of coastline between

Chile and Peru, including the Port of Antofagosta in present-day Peru. Once word was out that the Atacama Desert was rich in copper deposits and sodium nitrate—used for explosives, fertilizer, glass production and pottery enamel—the Europeans arrived, eager to exploit the area. Chileans decided they wanted it too.

The sparsely populated Atacama stretches 1,500 kilometres (1,000 miles) along the coast of South America. Although rich in minerals, it is one of the driest places on earth, averaging 2.5 centimetres (one inch) of rain per year, which means decades can pass without any moisture falling. The parched moonscape is hospitable only to birds that feast on the abundant offshore fish, nest along the rocky beaches, and drop their guano on the cliffs. Prisoners, poorly paid Indians and indentured Chinese "coolies" were forced to bag and load the bird droppings onto ships headed for Europe's agricultural areas to be used mostly as nitrate-rich fertilizers.

The War of the Pacific is also often referred to as the Saltpeter War (which, I suppose, historians decided sounds much better than the Shit War).

Borders in the lower populated areas of Bolivia were never precisely or legally established after independence. In 1866, a few years before the war, Chile and Bolivia had signed a treaty designating the 24th parallel—through the centre of the Atacama Desert—their legal boundary. The treaty also included a clause that gave Chile a share of the export taxes on minerals found in Bolivian territory and guaranteed no import taxes for Chilean mining companies.

As time passed, Bolivians resented sharing this money, which proved to be no paltry sum. They were also afraid that Chile, already leading in mineral extractions to the south, would seize Bolivia's mineral-rich holdings. To add to the paranoia, Peru was expanding its mining industry and wanted control of more coastal land. Fears were put to rest when Bolivia and Peru, in 1873, signed a secret alliance. The agreement guaranteed mutual military assistance to fight Chilean expansionism.

Three years after Bolivia and Peru signed their alliance, Hilarión Daza, a brutal and incompetent military leader, seized power in Bolivia. Daza, it might be added, started his life as a hoodlum in the streets of Sucre, specializing in petty theft. He honed his criminal skills in the military and perfected them during his stint in the presidency. He began his term by passing a liberal constitution—the ninth since independence—which protected property rights and economic concerns of the large silver industrialists. Although Daza faced serious opposition and many insurrections, he hoped to garner popularity by coercing concessions from Chile. He introduced a 10-cent export tax on every quintal (45 kilograms or 100 pounds) of nitrates mined by the British-Chilean Antofagasta Nitrate Company. Daza's tax netted some 28 million Bolivian pesos, 14 times the yearly budget. Chile's Antofagasta Nitrate & Rail Company refused to pay the tax, so the company was seized and set for auction. But on February 14, 1879, a Chilean force of 2,000 put a stop to the auction by occupying Antofagasta. Bolivia declared war. Peru was called to help Bolivia, and so Chile declared war on Peru as well.

Bolivia had no trained navy and Peru's antiquated ships were soon destroyed. Overland battles were just as lopsided and pitiful; the Chileans outnumbered both the Bolivian and Peruvian armies often as much as two to one, and occasionally more. Taking supplies over the Andes was cumbersome and, depending on the destination, often impossible, so the Chileans were able to restrict supplies from reaching their enemies by maintaining control of the seaways. On land, the Chileans marched methodically across the desert while the Bolivians and Peruvians could do nothing but leave a battery of minefields, cut the enemy's communication lines, and run.

After four years of war, Daza was overthrown in a well-planned coup led by the Bolivian liberals. He escaped to Europe with a fortune, most of which had been acquired through the nitrates export tax that he had originally introduced. Amazing as it sounds, Daza returned to Bolivia in 1894 hoping to absolve himself of any wrongdoing and regain the presidency. He was promptly murdered in the Uyuni train station a few days after entering the country. The blame was placed on President Mariano Baptista, but he was never convicted.

Bolivia's new government signed a truce with Chile and gave up the coastal province, including most of the Atacama Desert and the port of Antofagasta. This totalled one quarter of Bolivia's territory. The Treaty of Peace and Friendship, which pronounced Antofagasta Province permanently

96

Understanding Bolivia

Chilean, was signed in 1904 with the US assisting in the mediation process. The Bolivians wanted to do a side deal with Chile, hoping for a strip of land with a Pacific shoreline in occupied Peruvian territory. This deal was rejected. What they did get was a rail line between Oruro, through the old port of Antofagasta, to the newly built port at Arica in a part of Peru that was now occupied by Chile. Peru considered Bolivia's acceptance of this arrangement a betrayal; Peru didn't want to sacrifice coastal land and expected Bolivia to continue fighting to regain it.

Today, no matter what disputes arise with their powerful neighbours to the west, Bolivians always stand united on the desire to get the lost land back. They sometimes publish maps that include the lost turf, just as Guatemalan maps sometimes include Belize as a province. Bolivia also maintains a trained and waiting navy on Lake Titicaca to indicate they are ready at anytime to become a seafaring nation again. Some even say they have a submarine! How they figure to get this navy into the Pacific remains a state secret.

Eduardo Avaroa, a hero from the War of the Pacific, is remembered as saying, "Surrender? Only when you give up your grandmother!" The remark—still somewhat baffling to me—was made before he died in the Battle of Topàter on March 23, 1879. This is the fateful date on which Bolivia lost its land to Chile, and March 23 is still celebrated by Bolivians who vow each year to one day reclaim the lost land. I am sure this must make Chilean grandmothers feel insecure. If you are in Bolivia on March 23, take part in the celebrations, visit the naval base in Copacabana, and talk it up in support of regaining their coastal land. It'll earn you tons of free *chicha*.

Aniceto Arce Ruiz

The War of the Pacific had discredited the army, so governmental power switched from military *caudillos* to rich Creoles with financial ties to the mining industry. Two parties, the liberals and the conservatives, emerged after the war, although both had the same upper-class base and industrialist interests, much like liberals and conservatives of modern politics.

The first president of note to emerge from the new oligarchy was Aniceto Arce who, after the 1884 elections, made a backroom deal with Gregorio Pacheco, a silver magnate like Arce. At the time, Pacheco was the head of a

The lowering of the flag and the changing of the guard occurs daily at sunset on Plaza Murillo in La Paz. Uniforms from the War of the Pacific are worn by the guards.

faction of the conservative party and Arce was the leader of the main conservative party. The deal cemented the different factions, which resulted in the successful election of Pacheco as president and Arce as vice-president.

Little is known of Aniceto Arce before he became the 26th president in 1888. During his presidency, he was repressive and unsympathetic to Indians, which was consistent with the business oligarchy and remained so through the rest of the 19th and into the 20th century. The Indians were considered "communal" (read: Communist) and any attempt they made to band together was seen as a threat to cheap labour.

However, Arce brought many modern conveniences to Bolivia—electricity to La Paz, and the first steam engine to Pulacayo, where he owned the Huanchaca Mining Company's operations at the second-largest silver mine in the world. Although Pulacayo is mostly a deserted city today, Arce's mansion, now a museum, sits like a crown on a thorn bush overlooking the hovels and decaying buildings of Bolivia's first smelters and alpaca wool-spinning mills. In fact, the entire town is essentially a museum, with overgrown playgrounds, abandoned machinery and decrepit rail yards. Look for the ancient wood-burning trains, including one full of bullet holes supposedly from the guns of vigilantes chasing Butch Cassidy and the Sundance Kid. (See Chapter 8, "Famous Visitors.") Pulacayo is a popular destination for train buffs, but staying in the town of less than 500 miners isn't much fun and the accommodations are basic.

The Mesa de Plata and Porco mines, also owned by the Arce family, are located in the cone of a volcano between Potosi and Pulacayo. Production was profitable until 1959, and Arce's company usually employed between 20,000 and 30,000 people. If you visit Pulacayo, be sure to check out the cemetery: one of Arce's employees was a Scottish mining engineer named Bill Bailey who, as his tombstone reads, was killed in an underground explosion in 1910. I always wondered why Bill Bailey wouldn't come home. (Jazz enthusiasts will recognize the name from the 1902 Dixieland song, "Won't You Come Home Bill Bailey.")

Development of this mine gave Bolivia an economic boom that allowed for industrial modernization: new machines, a silver smelting company, foreign investment, professional banking systems and a rail line linking Pulacayo to Antofagasta on the Pacific. This line ran to Oruro and, as per the peace deal with Chile, the Oruro line ran to the Pacific. Foreign investment brought industrialists ready to rape the land of copper, lead, zinc and tin. This gave the upper crust a prosperous few years.

The train in Pulacayo was shot up by vigilantes chasing Butch Cassidy who, at the time, was riding the boxcar.

Arce's rail line helped make mining viable. On the downside, this same rail line allowed Chilean wheat to arrive at prices cheaper than any produced in Bolivia, which financially crippled the local farmers—mostly the indigenous population. Expansion of the haciendas on indigenous land resulted in Indians migrating to the cities, causing a huge unaddressed poverty problem. The urban slums didn't really show up on the country's books, and those in power—who bothered only with foreign investment—were unconcerned.

Arce knew that military strength was necessary for survival of the country and for protection of his interests. He reopened the military academy that had been closed since 1847 under Ballivián and had it relocated from Sucre to La Paz. He also brought in the draft service and established a school for noncommissioned officers. The new army was led by men not connected to the *caudillos*, though the new officers still knew the tradition of rule by General. When fighting broke out with Brazil over rubber production in Acre Province, the army wasn't strong enough, and so Bolivia lost more land. Arce asked for help from France and Germany in training the army, which resulted in the soldiers having a Prussian appearance and demeanour: they were unquestioning of the military's values or methodology, and homogonous in their ethnic and economic background. (In other words, no Indians were allowed.)

After Arce's term as president he retired to his mansion in Pulacayo, where he died in 1906.

Ismael Montes Gamboa, the Great President

Born on October 5, 1861, in a rural area outside La Paz to a rich land-owning family, Ismael Montes Gamboa had a pleasant and uneventful upbringing. His father was a general and, under this influence, Montes studied at the Ayacucho Military College. Upon graduation he joined the prestigious Murillo Regiment that unsuccessfully defended the coast during the War of the Pacific. He fought beside Heliodoro Camacho, one of the founders of the Liberal Party.

After the war Montes left the military and earned his law degree from San Andres University. He then taught civil rights courses, and spent most of his spare time working for the Liberals. Because he preferred the military to professional or academic life, he re-entered the army and rose to the rank of general during the La Paz Rebellion of 1898–99. As a rather theatrical general who also exhibited the finesse of a lawyer, he won the attention of President Colonel José Manuel Pando, one of the first supporters of the Liberal Party. Pando awarded Montes the minister of war position after the uprising. At this time, Montes took time out of his ambitious life to marry his cousin, Doña Betsabe Montes. In 1903 he fought against Brazil for the rubber-rich province of Acre, which won him more admiration even though they ended up losing a large chunk of land to Brazil. With Pando's support, Montes won the 1904 presidential elections.

He is credited with settling the border disputes with Chile that had lingered since the end of the War of the Pacific, 25 years earlier. Although Montes was called "the great president" for finishing rail lines, building elementary schools, making civil marriages legal, passing religious tolerance laws, and adopting the gold standard and other economic reforms, accepting the terms of the peace treaty with Chile was an unpopular move.

Montes lost the 1909 election to Fernando Guachalla, but Guachalla died of natural causes before he was sworn in. This influenced congress to invalidate the election and extend Montes's presidency for a few months. Eliodoro Villazón was then elected and took office in August 1909. Montes became the foreign minister to England and then to France.

Montes returned to run in the 1913 elections. Though he was now unpopular with many Liberals, who showed their lack of confidence by defecting to the Conservative and Republican parties, Montes still won. But his third term was not as successful as his first and second. There was an attempted coup, peasants and workers demonstrated for more rights, and the economy deteriorated under the World War I-related recession.

The 1917 elections relieved Montes of his presidential duties, but he kept his fingers in the ruling pie until his opposition forced him into exile in France, where he lived from 1920 to 1928.

Returning yet again, after the Liberals regained popularity, Montes insisted on a military position during the Chaco War against Paraguay. He was now in his seventies and, luckily for him, he died soon after receiving his appointment. The Chaco War was an even bigger disaster than the wars with Chile and Brazil.

Losses from Wars

Bolivia's land mass has shrunk to half its original size since independence, mostly due to territorial aggression by neighbouring countries and poor administration by Bolivian presidents. Over 100,000 square kilometres (38,600 square miles) of the Amazon basin were given to Brazil by the dictator Melgarejo, several thousand square kilometres—plus access to the Pacific—were lost to Chile during the War of the Pacific, part of the Acre Province was ceded to Brazil in 1903, and 150,000 square kilometres (58,000 square miles) were lost to Paraguay during the Chaco War. At this rate, in another hundred years Bolivia will more than fulfill Queen Victoria's demand that the country disappear from the map.

7

BOLIVIA'S RAILWAYS

Most of Bolivia's history and politics is staged in the high mountain regions of the Altiplano, where the major economic influences are metals and minerals. In the tropical areas, rubber is often overlooked as an influential commodity. In fact, rubber was the reason that Bolivia lost part of Acre Province in 1903.

By 1839, American businessman Charles Goodyear had developed a system of treating rubber so it could support extreme pressures and temperatures. Production of rubber hoses, vehicle and bicycle tires, shoes, and shoe soles caused a huge demand for high-quality latex, the white creamy sap that flows from the abundant rubber trees all through the Amazon and then hardens into rubber. Latex prices were beginning to rise. The people of Acre, whose land had never been properly surveyed because no country had ever wanted to claim it, fought for independence from Bolivia between 1899 and 1903. The Acreans now felt they could live off the enormous income from rubber. But Brazil, Bolivia and Peru bordered Acre, and they all wanted a share of the wealth.

The dispute for independence was settled by the signing of the Treaty of Petropolis on November 11, 1903—the Acreans were sold down the Madeira River, as they say. The province was divided between the three countries, with Brazil getting the biggest portion and Peru taking a strip along its border. Bolivia received the land between the Abuna and Madeira rivers, plus two million British pounds. A promise to build a rail link between Riberalta on the Beni and Puerto Velho on the Madeira, which would give Bolivia access to the Atlantic via the Amazon, was also part of the agreement.

At the time the agreement was signed, the Bolivia Rubber Company raised two million dollars in the US to purchase six estates in the Bolivian Amazon. Each estate had about 600,000 trees, and each tree could produce six pounds of latex a year. High-quality latex sold for 40 cents a pound; that works out to US$1,440,000 per year. (Not a bad turnover considering a bricklayer or plasterer in the US at that time made 50 cents per hour. US construction labourers made 17 cents per hour, with a grand yearly average of about $535.)

In 1876, someone smuggled some rubber tree seeds out of the Amazon and planted them in England. But anyone who has been to England knows very well the climate is nothing like that of the Amazon, and the seeds never grew well. The experimental seeds were then taken to Asia where, because of a tropical humid climate, they grew as quickly as they did in the Amazon. By 1910 Asia was in on the industry and their plantations, which were easier to access due to their proximity to ocean ports, produced rubber at a cheaper price than Bolivia or Brazil. The American prices crashed shortly after and the Amazon was cut out of the market. Another boom occurred during World War I, but it was during World War II—after the bombing of Pearl Harbor and the Japanese attack on the Dutch East Indies, where rubber latex was produced—that production of cheap synthetic rubber became a necessity. With the encouragement of the US government, production in the States soon topped 800,000 tons a year, all but destroying the natural rubber market around the world. Today, a small amount of natural rubber is still used for some things, such as airplane tires.

The drop in natural rubber markets forced rubber barons like Nicolas Suarez Callau to earn a living at cattle ranching or farming Brazil nuts. Other barons who'd gone to the Amazon basin to make a fortune—such as Frank Dunlevey with the Bolivia Rubber Company—had to pack up and return to the US.

Madeira–Mamoré Line

Transporting latex out of the jungle and across the Amazon basin to the Atlantic was easy from Brazil, but not from Bolivia. The overland routes were tedious and cumbersome, and both the workers and their donkeys were plagued with biting mosquitoes, tropical diseases, vicious snakes and a stifling climate. River transport was a better method.

Some rubber went from Bolivia's Acre Province up the Beni River a short distance by paddlewheelers (many wrecks of which can still be seen lying beside the riverbanks), and then by human packers up the rest of the Beni to Sorata where the rubber was loaded onto mules and sent by road to La Paz. From La Paz it was sent by rail to the Pacific, but this route was obviously too expensive.

Brazil has the Madeira River, wide and deep enough for barges and paddlewheelers. The Madeira goes down to Manaus on the Amazon River, and Manaus is accessible to ocean freighters. But the upper Madeira from Bolivia to the Brazilian town of Puerto Velho is treacherous with over 200 rapids and waterfalls along a 300-kilometre (200-mile) stretch. After Puerto

Tug boats pushing barges move freight and passengers up and down the Madeira River between Bolivia and Manaus, Brazil, on the Amazon River.

Velho it's smooth sailing down the Madeira to Manaus, and then out of the Amazon to the Atlantic.

The rubber barons decided that a railway around the rapids and waterfalls, from the Bolivian border town of Guayaramerín to Puerto Velho, was needed. In 1868 George Church, an American entrepreneur, surveyed the lands along the Madeira, formed a company, and obtained loans to finance the construction. But competitors kept the company in legal battles until, in 1879, Church abandoned the entire project.

After the Treaty of Petropolis was signed, construction of the rail line was awarded to another American entrepreneur named Percival Farquhar, who began the five-year, 367-kilometre-long (228-mile) project in August 1907. The heat, difficult terrain and raging malarial fevers caused an appallingly high number of deaths and drove up costs: the rail line cost about US$33 million and 3,600 lives by the time it was completed, one year before the price of rubber fell.

On the upside, the Madeira–Mamoré line operated until 1972 and today offers rail buffs a great display of historical cars and engines at the

Train barn at Puerto Velho on the Madeira River at the Bolivian/Brazil border.

museum in the train station in Puerto Velho. The roundhouse has probably 20 engines and cars dating as far back as the 1950s, but signage and historical data is lacking. There is also a Bolivian museum at the end of the rail line at Guayaramerín but it has just two old engines and some dusty documents.

Today there is a paved road from Puerto Velho along the Madeira River to Guayaramerín. A trip collecting commodities along the Madeira all the way to the Amazon River is the real draw. Tourists can travel this route on a riverboat collecting rubber, or more likely Brazil nuts, from communities between Puerto Velho and Manaus. It's actually a relaxing ride that only costs US$50 a week including all your meals and transportation costs. The trip takes around eight days, depending on how often your captain stops to load up more beer. As I mentioned before, these voyages are "BYOH"—bring your own hammock. A big advantage is that the trips are not too popular with foreigners yet, so you could be the only passenger.

Antofagasta–Bolivia Line

On the other side of the country, the Antofagasta–La Paz railway was started in 1872 when the port city of Antofagasta still belonged to Bolivia. Melbourne Clarke & Co. had constructed a short line from the nitrate mines in the foothills down to the coast. Mules powered the first cars. After steam engines were introduced in 1876, the track was lengthened eastward into the mountains. But Bolivia lost the coastal province of Antofagasta in the War of the Pacific, which ended in 1884. To appease the Bolivians, Chile granted access to the port and promised to continue the line to La Paz via Oruro.

Construction on the extension started in 1889 after funds were raised on the London Stock Exchange. By 1892 a narrow gauge line ran from Antofagasta to Uyuni (near Pulacayo), Oruro, Cochabamba and Potosi. By 1908 it went all the way to La Paz. Tin barons, with the support of Bolivian President Ismael Montes, helped pay for branch lines between the mines and the main track. Originally the narrow gauge was 76 centimetres (54 inches) wide and climbed 5,000 metres (15,000 feet) from the sea. The track was later replaced with the wider one (101.5 centimetres or 39.4

inches) and heavier engines were used to pull bigger cars. The line originally handled two million tons of freight per year and included 1,537 kilometres (955 miles) of track, including branch lines. Passenger service that included luxury sleeping and dining cars was added after World War I.

Bolivia is a country full of old trains, and there are plenty of organized tours of the rail lines and roundhouses of both Bolivia and Peru. For those interested in rail travel, a stop in Oruro, Potosi, Pulacayo, or Viachi on the Altiplano or at Guaqui on Lake Titicaca will reveal some old treasures, most of which are engines (with some in fairly decent shape).

If you're travelling to Uyuni to see the salt lake, most of the four-day tours include a stop at the Cementario del Trains located on the outskirts of town. If a section man is around, you may also hand-pump a small car for a few hundred feet along the track south of Uyuni. El Cementario del Trains features old wood-burning engines and tiny wood cars lined up along the rail line, looking like they've just been stopped by raiding bandits. Some cynics call this "the bag cemetery" because of all the garbage from Uyuni blowing around the rusting engines.

El Alto–Titicaca Line

The Ferrocarril Guaqui a La Paz (FCG) was built in 1903 and ran 95 kilometres (60 miles) between El Alto (above La Paz) to the Peruvian border on Lake Titicaca. At the lake, passengers and freight were transferred to British-made boats and transported to Puno, where they were again loaded onto rail cars and taken over to Arequipa. In 1904, the FCG purchased three electric engines and four trams and built the electric railway—nine kilometres (5.5 miles) from El Alto to the centre of La Paz. This section had a perilously steep grade, and trains often jumped the rails—sometimes killing the passengers.

Because electricity was not very reliable in Bolivia, steam engines were an improvement over the electric engines. In 1913, a new wide-gauge line was built to the centre of the city, with steam engines pulling the freight. As technology advanced, steam engines were replaced by diesels, but in the mid-1950s all lines into the city centre were closed.

Santa Cruz Line

This line was built in 1909 and runs about 750 kilometres (500 miles) to Puerto Suarez along the Pantanal near the Brazil, Paraguay and Bolivia border. Terminal Bimodal, a bus and train station in Santa Cruz, is huge and modern with regular daily service in every direction. Most tourists use this station to depart for trips to the missions. Once extensive repairs are needed, however, it will probably be abandoned, thus joining other Cementarios del Trains like those at Pulacayo and Uyuni. Closures such as this will only add to Bolivia's transport problems. Visitors discover right away that transportation in Bolivia is dangerous: roads are hazardous, the national airline has collapsed, bus accidents kill thousands yearly, and no foreigner in his right mind would rent a car. On the other hand, rail repair is expensive and not something in which the government has wanted to invest—up until now.

End of the Railways

Bolivia's government-owned rail lines have fallen into serious disrepair. According to a study done by the Japanese for the World Bank, it would take 30 years and US$46 billion to repair the 4,000-kilometre (2,500-mile), single-track lines. The western section of these lines connects La Paz with Cochabamba, Sucre, Potosi and Uyuni. A second line branches over the Andes to Arica and Antofagasta in Chile and a third line runs through the foothills to Argentina. The eastern lines connect Santa Cruz with Sao Paulo in Brazil and with Argentina. Connecting Cochabamba to Santa Cruz has been unsuccessfully tried numerous times. Under pressure from the World Bank, the rail lines were privatized in 1995. The Bolivian government signed an agreement with a Chilean company that was partnered with some American companies. The Chileans purchased controlling shares of all the lines. According to the agreement, Bolivia was to repair and maintain the lines at a cost of US$1 billion, and the Chileans and Americans would supply only technical assistance. Once upgraded, private American and Chilean rail companies would run the system transporting freight and passengers to the Pacific. They would also collect the revenue. But this did not work; Bolivia has never been able to maintain a paying rail service, and the Americans and Chileans were also unable to make what they would call a reasonable profit.

Many lines closed. The line from La Paz to Antofagasta fell under control of the wealthy Luksik family in Chile, which also owns interests in soda pop, cars and advertising in Bolivia.

The present government is implementing the National Development Plan in an attempt to negotiate a fair deal for regained management of the rail lines by purchasing the controlling shares before 2010. Meanwhile, Chile doesn't want to lose its Bolivian line, knowing that there are profits to be made from the transportation of the gas reserves so abundant in the Santa Cruz region. The story plays like a soap opera—all we can do is tune in each year to see if new players are in the act and if anything is happening.

8

FAMOUS VISITORS

Colonel Percy Harrison Fawcett

In 1906, British adventurer Colonel Percy Harrison Fawcett was hired by the Royal Geographic Society to help settle the border between Brazil and Bolivia in the Amazon Basin. He accepted the job because he was bored with military life. Fawcett was a tall, well-built man who excelled in almost everything he tried, from soldiering and engineering to sports, and reached the position of colonel by age 19. He had worked in Hong Kong and then Ceylon (present-day Sri Lanka), where he met and married his wife, whom he affectionately called "Cheeky." By his mid-twenties, Fawcett had designed and built a yacht he called the *Icthoid Curve*, faster by many knots than any other cutter of that time. He had also worked with the British secret service in North Africa, but was drawn to the Amazon.

Fawcett's Bolivian journey began along a donkey path that visitors can still travel today. Within 100 kilometres (60 miles), Fawcett's route to the Amazon—better known as the Mapiri Trail—drops 4,000 metres (12,000 feet) from a pass near the mountain village of Sorata down to sea level on the Mapiri River. The trail then follows the shores of the Mapiri (a tributary of the Beni) where travellers brave mud, bugs, bats, anacondas and—as one

recent group found out after losing tens of thousands of dollars' worth of camera equipment—some not-so-welcoming locals. The trail was originally developed by slaves carrying rubber from the rubber plantations in the Amazon to Sorata, where the rubber was then placed on pack animals and transported to La Paz. It was a tough haul. It took two hours to go six kilometres (four miles) and pack animals managed to go only 10 metres (30 feet) before having to rest.

Besides being an adventurer, Fawcett was also into the occult. For this he was often ridiculed, but his

Percy H. Fawcett, 1911 in Pelechuco. *Archive photo*

unorthodox interests earned him the friendship of fellow Brit Sir H. Rider Haggard, author of *King Solomon's Mines* and other Victorian adventure stories of hidden civilizations in Africa or the Amazon. Haggard told Fawcett about a mythical city in the Amazon, and Fawcett was inspired. The city, called El Dorado, was tucked somewhere into the jungle and had golden temples and white-haired rulers. Melchior Dias Moreyra, a half-Portuguese, half-Indian man, was supposedly the first to find it. He was the son of a Tupinambas Indian maiden and had become better known by his Indian name, Muribeca. Legend has it that after Muribeca accumulated huge amounts of gold, silver and precious stones in El Dorado, he sailed for Portugal, settled down, and eventually told his son, Roberio Dias, his tale of the hidden city.

In 1610, so the story goes, Roberio—with his father's directions to the treasure sealed in his mind—went to negotiate with the king of Portugal. The greedy king agreed to finance an expedition to El Dorado. In exchange for the gold Roberio vowed to find, the king promised him the title of "Marquis das Minas" and sealed the commission in an envelope to be handed over only after the location of the treasure was revealed. On the voyage to

New Spain, a distrusting Roberio bribed the officer holding the commission. When he opened it, Roberio found to his dismay that he was to be made a captain of the army rather than a marquis. He then refused to reveal the location of the treasures, so the captain of the boat returned to Spain and had Roberio incarcerated. Two years later, Roberio purchased his freedom and was released from jail. He lived a quiet life and died without ever disclosing the directions his father had entrusted to him. Numerous parties have tried to reach El Dorado since then, but all have failed.

So it happened that Percy Harrison Fawcett was exploring Bolivia with two goals in mind: surveying, and looking for a legend. When he got to the Beni, he found nothing of the lost city. But after completing his survey project, he decided to try again.

He left for England, resigned from the military, and returned to the Amazon. He went into the jungle again and again, but on each expedition he failed to find the city. And every time he returned to England, he was mobbed by reporters. Some say Fawcett's reports to the Geographic Society and the stories published in the British newspapers inspired Sir Arthur Conan Doyle to write the book *Lost World*. Mount Roraima in Venezuela and Noel Kempff Mercado Park in eastern Bolivia also lay claim to the setting of Doyle's story; either way, in South America it seems that adventure inspires adventure.

On his final journey (which was his sixth or seventh attempt), Fawcett took his 22-year-old son Jack and Jack's friend Raleigh Rimmell with him. Fawcett now believed the lost city was in the swampy Mato Grosso region in present-day Brazil. After sending his wife a telegram on May 29, 1925, saying everything looked normal and inviting, they sailed down the Rio Verde, a small tributary of the Amazon dotted with treacherous rapids. They were never heard from again, and no traces of them or their vessel were ever found.

There have been 13 known expeditions into the area in search of Fawcett, and more than 100 rescuers have died trying to find him. The people who lost the camera equipment on the Mapiri trail were adventurers trying to follow in Fawcett's footsteps. Kalapalo Indians held them hostage for several days until they were set free in exchange for their expensive gear.

Percy James Boland

Unlike adventurers, immigrants have for the most part been welcomed by the Bolivian government—especially those immigrants with light skin, money, and technological or scientific knowledge. Born Patrick James in Australia in 1886, Percy James Boland was an inventor who, in 1912, travelled to Santa Cruz via San Francisco, California and Buenos Aires. From Buenos Aires to Santa Cruz, he drove the first motor vehicle ever seen in Bolivia. This adventure took six months along horrendous roads and across open country. It wasn't until the mid-1950s that roads and rail lines were completed, joining Santa Cruz to the rest of the country.

Upon arrival, Boland fell in love with Santa Cruz and settled down. He married a Bolivian, started a family, and opened the city's first mechanics' workshop. To counter the heat, he developed the first ice factory and sold the ice for iceboxes, the precursors to refrigerators. He started Santa Cruz's first public power plant, and connected some homes to the lighting system. He also built the first swimming pool and was involved in construction of the city's first oil refinery.

Boland's story ends happily, but his descendents didn't do too well. His son, Hernan, was released as a prisoner of war after the Chaco War ended and received the Chaco War Medal of Honour. He joined the Workers' Union that amalgamated with the MNR under the leadership of Victor Paz Estenssoro. (See "Prelude to Revolution" in Chapter 10.) When that government fell, Hernan escaped to Argentina with nothing; his personal belongings and bank accounts were confiscated by the government. His story shows what so often happens to those who fall in love with Bolivia—they live well until the political winds shift, and those who were successful one moment are penniless the next.

Trail of Butch Cassidy

Some characters arrive on the Bolivian stage while on the run from the law. Cassidy and Sundance, actual outlaws immortalized on screen as popular icons of the American West, are just two examples of being on the lam in Bolivia.

Butch Cassidy was born Robert Leroy Parker in Utah on April 13, 1866, to Mormon parents. Ten years before Robert's birth, his grandfather had walked partway across the US leading faithful followers to Salt Lake City. Robert's father Max, who was 12 years old at the time, helped his mother bury his father (Robert's grandfather) after he froze to death during a bitter cold night. Max was deeply affected by the loss of his father and his impoverished upbringing—the root of his later insistence that his own children learn to work hard and earn an honest living so that they would never have to know that type of hardship. Robert got the "earn money" part right, and he did indeed work hard at what he did, but apparently the "honest living" part didn't register.

As a youngster Robert worked on the farm and then in a butcher shop, hence his nickname (nicknames were popular in those days). The name Cassidy was taken on later, in honour of his early childhood hero and cattle rustler, Mike Cassidy. Butch's sidekick, Sundance Kid (born Harry Alonzo Longabaugh), got his name from the prison where he spent his first and only jail sentence: Sundance, Wyoming.

Shortly after Sundance was released from prison in the mid-1880s, he and the handsome Butch met and rode out looking for loose women and strong whisky. But their vices didn't come free, so they teamed up with Tom McCarty, Matt Warmer and Bart Madden in 1889 and pulled a bank job in Telluride, Colorado. They netted US$10,000. It was Butch's initiation into a new career of large-scale bank and payroll heists, and he continued to practise and refine his profession for the next 19 years.

In 1894 Butch was caught for horse rustling and spent a few months in prison, where he hit it off with Kid Curry. Together they formed the Wild Bunch, a motley crew of 20 card sharks, gunslingers and sporting house gals. The American West was still wild and dangerous with few law enforcement officers, a perfect place for Butch to hone his skills.

By 1897 the Pinkerton Bounty Hunters were looking for the Wild Bunch who, to prevent detection, then disbanded. Butch and Sundance, now each with a price of US$4,000 on his head, rode to Mexico. The Pinkerton agents followed, so Butch and Sundance continued south by boat and eventually settled in Argentina in 1901, where they purchased a ranch near Cholila and tried to lead a crime-free life. In 1905, Butch and Sundance were tipped off that the Pinkerton hunters were in Argentina looking for them, so they pulled a few heists and crossed into Chile. By now it was 1906.

Etta Parker, a schoolteacher in the movie but a prostitute and girlfriend of Sundance in real life, had joined them in Argentina. But Etta was tired of living on the run, so she left for California while Sundance and Butch pulled off a slew of robberies. When things got too hot in Chile, they crossed into Bolivia.

In the Hollywood version, this is where Butch says to Sundance, "So, when I say Bolivia, you just think California. You wouldn't believe what they're finding in the ground down there. They're just fallin' into it. Silver mines, gold mines, tin mines, payrolls so heavy we'd strain ourselves stealin' em."

The two robbed a bank in Eucalyptus, not far over the Bolivian border and then hit a payroll train. With their pockets lined, they got honest jobs and started working for the Concordia Tin Mines near Tupiza, where they became respected community members.

But Butch liked his booze, which always loosened his tongue. He often bragged about the jobs he'd pulled. The locals became suspicious, but did nothing about it.

Working for the mining company gave Butch and Sundance inside information as to when and by which route the payroll trains would arrive. It was in the Plaza of Tupiza that they made their plans to rob the Chocaya Tin and Silver Mine payroll. If you make it to Tupiza, sit in the plaza and instead of plotting a robbery, imagine a trip of your own along the Butch Cassidy Trail. Local guides will provide horse, hat and hundreds of tales about the bandits as you ride.

After this minor heist, the robbers visited a Scottish mining engineer who lived in Verdugo, about 20 kilometres (12 miles) south of Tupiza. They drank beer and, unbeknownst to the engineer, planned a robbery at the Tupiza bank. Once in town they learned that the Bolivian army was guarding the bank, so they backed off and switched their interests to the Ayamaro payroll due the following day.

On November 3, 1908, while the morning mist was still on the fields, Butch and Sundance followed the caravan snaking its way up the Vaca

Then as now, horses are the best mode of transportation in Butch Cassidy Country.

Huañusca Pass from the Ayamaro Hacienda in the village of Salo. Masked and with guns drawn, they rode up to the caravan, politely asked for the saddle bags, which the mule train captain handed over, and rode off. But the captain recognized their Yankee accents and once he got to Tupiza, he fingered them to the miners.

Since it was their wages going over the hill, the robbed miners formed a posse, telegraphed the border guards to tell them to watch for the gringos, and joined the army that was already on the trail of the two bandits.

Butch and Sundance returned to their Scottish friend in Verdugo who, by then, suspected who they were and extracted a confession. Butch and Sundance headed into the mountains toward Uyuni, crossed a pass and then stopped to eat and change horses at a farm near San Vicente. But when they paid in large bills, acted nervous, and asked many questions, including border-crossing particulars, the farmer became suspicious. He told Butch he was going into town to purchase more beer, but fetched the army instead.

From the farmhouse window, Butch saw the army approach and started shooting. One soldier fell and the battle began in earnest. Darkness descended, a scream and two shots were heard, and then all went silent.

The following morning, an officer called through the door of the farmhouse but received no response. Cautiously entering, he found Sundance shot numerous times, with the fatal bullet—probably delivered by Butch—lodged in his head. Near him lay Butch with a bullet hole at his temple. The manhunt was over. The two were buried in Bolivia, although there are other theories as to what happened to them. Some go as far as to say they got back to the US and lived long, quiet lives.

Although DNA analysis of bodies in the San Vicente cemetery at the supposed burial site has been conducted, identification of Butch and Sundance remains unconfirmed. A crude wooden cross that simply says *"fallecer"* (passed away) is taken by locals and travellers alike to represent their grave.

True fans of the Robert Redford and Paul Newman movie can take a horse tour along the same route Butch and Sundance took, from the main plaza in Tupiza and through the dry desert-like mountains to St. Vincente. The scenery is captivating, the ride is hot and dusty, and the historical farmhouse where the shootout took place has been preserved.

9

MINING BARONS

Tin Men Trinity

At the beginning of the 20th century, rubber and silver prices dropped, and tin took over the world market just in time to keep the Bolivian government and Hidalgo white-collar economy going. Europe's tin production was declining and new uses for tin were discovered every day. Mines like Pulacayo were a huge success, as were Potosi and Oruro, in providing minerals and metals such as zinc, lead, bismuth, copper and tin.

Farther south, toward Argentina, mining companies moved into the Tupiza area and extracted silver, tin, antimony and lead. During the late 1800s, the Concordia Tin Mine, the Compaño de Aramayo, and the Chocaya Mining Company became exceptionally big. This attracted international interests. Rail lines were added to the existing Potosi–La Paz–El Alto lines to get the ore out.

The powerful mine owners benefited from low labour costs in Bolivia. The three most influential mining barons were Simón Patiño, a poor Indian who rose like bread dough in the financial world, Carlos Victor Aramayo, an elite member of a wealthy mining family, and Mauricio Hochschild, a rich German immigrant and agnostic Jew.

Although they didn't take direct roles in government, the three influenced those in power to ensure unregulated foreign exchange, abundant money for exploration and development, and low taxation on minerals. During the last years of the 19th century, this resulted in a constant—but tolerated—budget deficit and a rather peaceful, albeit short, period of stable government.

Miners were finally working for sufficient wages that gave them and their families regular meals and half-decent houses. This kept peasant opposition to government practices at bay. But when metal prices kept increasing and the wages didn't, the

Oruro, close to where Patiño made his first strike, is still dependent on mining. Unionized miners here overthrew the army and set up a short-lived social-democratic government in 1952.

miners got restless. Strikes and protests—put down by the government—were especially common during World War I. The miners in turn formed a Marxist party, Partido de la Izquierda Revolucionaria (PIR); a socialist party called Movimiento Nacionalista Revolucionario (MNR); and the Argentinean-financed Logia Rason de Patrea (RADEPA). By the beginning of the 1940s, the three leftist groups were calling for nationalization of the mines and freedom for the Indians. Supporters demonstrated in La Paz. The movement rapidly took hold in Oruru and Pulacayo and then on to every Hidalgo estate in the country. By late 1943, revolution was brewing.

Tradition of Protest

Remember that Bolivian colonial history began with exploitation of the mines and miners in Potosi—it's an important factor in modern Bolivian politics and contemporary Bolivian culture. Today, when foreign companies attempt a takeover of natural resources such as water or gas, the response is instant. Unrelenting demonstrations led by the mostly indigenous

Nice view for Pulacayo miners buried near their place of employment.

population usually turn violent: under government orders, the military and police shoot tear gas and rubber or real bullets and beat demonstrators with truncheons, while the protestors fight back by building road blocks and throwing stones. It is this historical background and tradition of protest that sheds light on the political progress Bolivian Indians, now governed by indigenous president Evo Morales, have made in recent years.

Victor Carlos Aramayo

Victor Carlos Aramayo inherited his fortune from his father Felix, who had inherited it from his father José Avelino, known as the father of Bolivian capitalism. José Avelino was born near Potosi in 1809 and came from a debt-riddled landowning background that forced him to work at a young age instead of studying. Out of necessity he became a cunning entrepreneur and opened a much-needed shop selling European goods. He invested his profits in mines, and his offspring continued to successfully expand the family fortune. A dynasty was born.

Because he had known poverty, José Avelino built decent housing and schools for the children of his workers and brought in foreign teachers. Despite his own lack of education, he also wrote many books about commerce, economics and politics in a simple yet compelling style. He became Bolivia's first self-made millionaire and then entered politics as a congressman and close adviser to President Linares. Upon José Avelino's death in 1882, his son Felix successfully continued the business and in turn passed it onto his son, Victor Carlos. After finishing his Oxford education, Victor Carlos worked the family business with the same integrity as his predecessors.

By Victor Carlos's reign, the Aramayos owned 25 percent of Bolivia's mining industry. They kept their headquarters in Bolivia and retained control of their business, even though it was heavily financed by foreign investment. The Aramayos's Socavón Mine in Oruro has a simple cathedral over the mineshaft. The cathedral, constructed in 1881, now houses the Virgin of Socavón, considered the patron saint of miners. In one of the tunnels—accessed from the cathedral—is a museum that contains office equipment and documents used during the early 1900s.

Victor Carlos also furthered the family legacy by founding *La Razon de La Paz*, a newspaper known for its editorial fairness and technological superiority. He used it to advocate right-wing political issues and financial matters important to the mining industry. The paper was confiscated, along with his mines, during the 1952 revolution.

Of the three tin families, the Ayamaros are still liked best for their integrity, philanthropy and dedication to Bolivia. There is a statue of Victor Carlos in the main plaza in Tupiza.

Simón Patiño

Simón Patiño was born in 1860 (though some sources say 1862) in Cochabamba to a humble Indian family. He married Alvina Rodriques, a peasant from Oruro, then the second largest city in the country. Oruro was—and still is—rich in minerals, but at the time of Patiño's marriage, the economy was depressed. Silver was running out and the tin boom had not yet started.

Patiño began his mining career as a clerk at Huanchaca, the mine owned by president Aniceto Arce Ruiz. He moved up the ranks to become a mineral purchaser for the German Fricke Mining Company in Oruro, where he learned the financial ins and outs of the industry. Luck struck when a friend to whom Patiño had lent money was unable to pay. In exchange for the debt, he gave Patiño a deed to his mine on Llallagua Mountain south of Oruro.

But claim jumping was common in those days, and Patiño often had to defend his company in court. This was no easy task for an Indian at that time; according to the constitution drawn up by Santa Cruz, Indians were non-persons and courts were forbidden to recognize their claims. It was often easier to settle a dispute with guns. In 1901, just a year after Patiño obtained the mine, a neighbouring miner, Armando Artigue, tried to claim jump. The wild-west gun battle, with each side heavily armed and popping away at each other, almost ended in death for Artigue. Patiño kept his claim.

Patiño worked hard on his mine but had no results for three long years. At one low point he had to sneak away at the end of the day because he couldn't pay his helpers. However, less than a year after that, one of his helpers ran from the mine yelling that he'd found a huge vein of silver. Patiño's wife Alvina, who had been working with them, fell on her knees and prayed that it would turn out to be tin, and not silver. Somehow, the Patiños seemed instinctively to know that tin would be the most important metal of the 20th century.

The vein indeed was tin, which doubled in price on the world market between 1896 and 1902, and then doubled again by 1912. Production increased ten-fold while exports multiplied by 18. Some veins found on Llallagua were three metres (10 feet) wide and the ore contained 65 percent tin, which meant the rock was so rich the tin didn't have to be concentrated before shipping. The Patiño mine was named La Salvadora (the saviour).

Patiño used his profits to purchase the near-depleted Uncia silver mine, which proved lucrative a short time later even with falling silver prices. He then purchased the British Uncia Mining Company and, in about 1920, the Chilean Llallagua Company, the other company working the mountain where he got his start. It eventually became the richest tin mine in the world, producing roughly 17 percent of the world's supply. With the purchase of Llallagua Company, Patiño controlled 50 percent of all the country's mining industry.

Patiño hired mining engineers to run the day-to-day operation of the mines, preferring instead to work on improving his operations by updating his technology. In 1901 he purchased a million-dollar, diesel-operated concentrating mill—the first in Bolivia—which quadrupled production within three years. In 1918 he purchased Bolivia's first generator, a Sulzer from Switzerland with a 600-horsepower motor. It was an updated one that, in my opinion, should still be used to supplement the country's sporadic electricity. He also opened the Banco Mercantil in Bolivia and his general manager, Charles Geddes, became his biographer. Geddes's book, *The Tin King*, was written from a pro-company standpoint. It was published in London in 1972 and can occasionally be found for about US$150 in second-hand bookstores.

In addition to rising metal and mineral prices, the 20th century brought a changing labour climate. Unions were starting to form, particularly in North America and Europe, but also in South America. The First National Congress of Workers met in La Paz in 1912; working conditions and housing concerns in the mining towns were the main source of disgruntlement. The number of mine workers had increased yearly, but the housing for the workers had not. Many of them were immigrants from surrounding countries and they were housed in one-room dwellings with only an outside kitchen. This caused family discord, which often carried over to the workplace. Strikes in mining towns increased throughout the country. On the other hand, it was imperative for Patiño to keep labour costs down. Although tin on the world market sold for 52 cents a pound, he had signed an agreement with the US to sell it for 40.5 cents a pound.

Rather than getting involved in politics, Patiño—along with the other barons—stayed away from the front line. Instead they hired good lawyers to challenge union opposition and to keep wages down, and they wooed politicians into keeping both mining taxes and workers' rights minimal. This group of lawyers, politicians and lobbyists was known as "la rosca," a popular term meaning "the screw." This meant that the miners and the politicians were being pressured into subservience by the barons.

But there was some slow progress for the miners. President Ismael Montes, who ruled for nine years at the start of the 20th century, tried to work against tin magnates like Patiño. Montes wanted to improve miners' working conditions. At the time, the wages were less than half of those in

Europe. Foreigners were also investing heavily in Bolivia's mining industry, but taking their huge profits home. Opposition from industry and military coups kept Montes from succeeding with his reforms.

Succeeding Montes at the beginning of 1917 was José Gutiérrez Guerra. During his reign, the mining industry helped pay for the expansion and development of the railway, army and other industrial infrastructure that was being partly subsidized by government. Gutiérrez took Patiño to court on a tax evasion charge hoping to extract more money, but Patiño had more money and power than the government and was able to beat the rap. He then used his fortune to subvert the Liberal Party and force Gutiérrez to abdicate.

Most years, Patiño spent half his time in Europe minding his finances and his contacts. While there he diversified and invested in mining and smelting companies in Germany, England, South Africa, Canada, the US, Europe and Southeast Asia. He ruled the European tin market. Before World War I, he was so respected in Germany that he was awarded the Red Eagle of Prussia and invited to dine with Kaiser Wilhelm.

World War II increased demand and upped prices. But back home discontent rose. When miners from Patiño's Catavi mine went on strike in 1943, Patiño asked the government for help—using his friend, US ambassador Pierrela Lagarde Boal, to apply extra pressure. Soldiers fired on the 8,000 strikers, killing 400, though some sources claim there were 700 killed. (Official records state that only 19 men were killed and 30 wounded—my guess is that the figures of 19 and 30 were the military casualties, not the miners.) The government announced at the end of the massacre that the leftist insurrection had been successfully controlled. In a way this was true, but miner resentment was boiling.

Patiño's mining success eventually made him one of the richest men in the world. They called him "Rey del Estaño" (the Tin King). But really, Patiño was more than a mining magnate. His business career proved that he and his wife were financial and management geniuses: yes, they bought mines, but they also purchased companies that refined, transported and marketed metals. They bought up banks that did the financing. They moved their business to Europe as soon as they could, away from the psychotic Creole generals and their erratic governments. They were also prudent financial planners, placing their companies under a directorship that took any real control away from their inexperienced, less business-savvy children. Patiño recognized the interconnections of democracy and business, and wisely put all his production in the hands of the Allies through both World Wars, despite the fact that the Kaiser and other German officials had courted his favour.

Patiño built mansions in Potosi, Oruro and Cochabamba. His manor in Oruro is in disrepair but is well worth an afternoon of exploring. Part of the interior design is French Provincial—popular at the time—complete with tapestry chairs and smoking rooms with painted ceilings depicting elegant women smoking. The game room is an exception, with a Middle Eastern decor including rich Persian carpets and ivory statues. The carriages are many and exquisite. One of them required ten horses to pull and Patiño insisted that the horses be white.

Though Patiño was known for this display of opulence and over-the-top luxury, the modern-day Patiño Foundation, formed by estate money, is an important and philanthropic contributor to Bolivian society. Every year it provides money for the sciences and for the performing arts, funding for Bolivian scholars studying at foreign universities (if they promise to return to Bolivia and work a minimum of six years), and bursaries for painters and sculptors. The foundation also supports a medical clinic, public housing and an experimental farm that has a genetic research centre for agricultural studies. The centre publishes books and maintains one of the larger libraries in the country.

Though the foundation headquarters are in France, the Bolivian office is housed in Patiño's Cochabamba mansion, which is also a

Patiño's mansion in Cochabamba is now used as a museum and cultural centre.

delight to visit. The mansion's exterior is French Provincial and its interior can only be called eclectic, a potpourri of architectural and decorative styles that don't really match well but are interesting all the same. For example, the heads of Roman emperors adorn the classical main salon and look a bit nervous under the Vatican-like dome, which features Christian angels. Upstairs in the study is a desk once used by Napoleon. There's also a very long and ornate bed in the master bedroom that was originally used by the Patiños, who were quite short,

Patiño had two Labrador dogs carved in stone as entrance pillars to his mansion in Cochabamba.

but the bed was extended two feet to accommodate Charles de Gaulle when he visited. The Cochabamba mansion shows that the Patiños were good-hearted as well as smart, despite their questionable esthetic taste: elsewhere on the estate grounds there's an outbuilding where peasants used to shower at no cost. Near the entry gates are two gigantic marble Labrador dogs with whisky barrels under their chins—Patiño loved the stories about St. Bernards rescuing people in the Alps, but his artist had probably never seen a St. Bernard.

The Patiños considered Europe far more sophisticated than Bolivia, and lived in Paris for a number of years before moving to New York and finally to Buenos Aires, where Simón died of a heart condition in 1947. (He did have a short interlude in Bolivia in his old age, but the high altitude was far too difficult to endure with his weakening heart.) Patiño was a striver when it came to social status. His children were married off to impecunious and inbred remnants of European aristocracy. The oldest son, Antenor, married Doña Maria Christina de Borbon y Bosch-Labrus, the Duchess of Durcal. Historians speculate that this showed Patiño's deep insecurity as a Bolivian, or maybe the marriages were his proof of victory over those who had long oppressed his own people.

Maruicio (Moritz) Hochschild

Born in Biblis, a village close to Frankfurt, Germany, in 1881, Moritz Hochschild was the son of Jeanette Hirsch and Ludwik Hochschild, a middle-class Jewish merchant who, through good business practices, had acquired bourgeois status. Although Moritz never earned his doctorate as a young man, he trained as a mining engineer in Freiberg, as did his two brothers. He then worked in Spain, Australia and South America, finally starting a mine in Chile. He re-wrote his doctorial thesis in 1921, after he had worked in the field for some time, and the thesis was accepted. Moritz then became Dr. Hochschild to most, and "Don Mauricio" (his name in Spanish) to his friends and acquaintances. "Don Mauricio" was a big, bald-headed man with heavy brown eyebrows and a grand stomach on which he dropped Havana cigar ashes and bits of food from his enormous meals.

During World War I, Hochschild returned to Germany from Chile and escaped front-line duty by working for the war effort finding and extracting metals. After the war he and his brother expanded their own mining company in Chile and moved into Peru and Bolivia, where Hochschild first learned to admire Patiño's versatility. Hochschild opened Mauricio Hochschild & Co. in 1923, the same year Patiño left.

Hochschild began by modernizing and reworking abandoned tin mines and then rapidly diversified into mining copper, zinc, silver and tungsten. Some Bolivians welcomed Hochschild while others cursed him as just another greedy capitalist. He hobknobbed with the Aramayos and he dabbled in politics by entertaining powerful friends who might be able to keep miners' wages and living standards low. He wasn't as culturally sophisticated as the Aramayos or as socially ambitious as the Patiños, but he always displayed impeccable manners. His generosity to the Catholic Church and to his family members during the Nazi era in Germany was legendary within his circles, and he spent over a million dollars of his own money relocating about 2,000 Jews to the foothills of the Andes. He also set some of them up in businesses.

It must be noted that Jews had been immigrating to South America since the Inquisition in the 1600s, but their welcome waned just before World War II. Considering Bolivia's right-of-right-wing political tendencies, Hochschild's heroic and dangerous efforts are commendable.

Between the wars, Hochschild's co-barons moved all their financial holdings to Europe, but Hochschild had adopted Bolivia as his home and believed staying was what he should do. It proved to be a bad move.

Because of his non-pretentiousness, and possibly because he was a Jew (his brother's family in America worked very hard at appearing non-Jewish), Hochschild wasn't respected by many politicians, journalists or powerful businessmen. Patiño, who experienced prejudice as an Indian, could have told him that these were not nice guys, and they didn't like nice guys like Don Mauricio. President Germán Busch slapped Hochschild in jail in 1939 and would've shot him were it not for powerful intervention by the US and Argentina. During the 1943 to 1946 reign of fascist Gualberto Villaroel, Hochschild was again jailed for plotting against the government, but international pressure, especially from Chilean ambassador Benjamin Cohen, resulted in his release. He was then kidnapped by a group of Bolivian army officers who had pledged to dispose of all active opponents to the new regime. Under international pressure (and possibly a few bucks' ransom from the family), this too ended in Hochschild's freedom. But upon his release in 1944, he was strongly encouraged to flee Bolivia, and he did, leaving most of his assets in the country and his business under the care of Bolivian management. He controlled these assets from Chile.

All mining companies, including those of Patiño and Aramayo, were confiscated during the 1952 revolution, but Hochschild was the only employer to guarantee his staff employment. From Chile, he ensured that the miners became state employees and that the staff and administrators were relocated to Brazil, Peru, Chile and Argentina to work for other Hochschild enterprises. When his personal possessions were confiscated, there was little of value found in his modest apartment.

Hochschild died in Paris in 1965 of natural causes. Today, his greatnephew, Adam Hochschild, is an award-wining American journalist and activist who founded *Mother Jones* magazine.

THE CHACO WAR (1932–35)

During the world depression of the 1930s, Bolivia was, like most countries, in turmoil. To add to its distress, Bolivia and Paraguay let their usual play-fighting on the border get out of hand. At the beginning of the 20th century, Paraguay controlled a large portion of the Chaco Boreal, 260,000 square kilometres (100,000 square miles) of flatland covered mostly with scrub brush suitable for ranching or growing coca, then a mainstay of the Paraguayan economy. It is an isolated area bordered by the Pilcomayo River to the southwest and the Paraguay River to the northeast. The two rivers join at Asunción and flow into the Atlantic at Buenos Aires. The climate is humid and hot in summer, but cold and windy in winter. An important fact to know about the region is that there is little potable water.

Paraguay and Bolivia, both land-locked countries, needed control of the Paraguay River to make exporting economically viable. When Standard Oil of New Jersey, a company started by the Rockefellers, went into the area in the early 1920s to explore for oil, the pressure to improve access to the Atlantic increased. Bolivians believed the Chaco to contain huge oil reserves, so they listened to the oil company. On the other side of the border, Shell Oil was exploring in Paraguay and encouraging the Paraguayans to control the river.

On June 15, 1932, the Bolivian army—made up mostly of conscripted Indians from the Altiplano who preferred tending corn crops to fighting—attacked Paraguay at Fort Vangaurdia. The Paraguayan army, accustomed to guerilla-style warfare and the sweltering jungle heat of the Chaco, readily protected their country from the aggressors.

The Bolivians seized many Paraguayan strongholds such as Fort Boqueron, but soon lost them again. German General Hans von Kundt, who was responsible for training Bolivian troops, was brought in to lead the attack on Fort Nanawa, where they fought for several months. Kundt was a good organizer but poor leader and tactician. He didn't seem to worry about the slaughter of his Indian troops until he started running out of them.

Finding water and drilling wells was crucial. When water was scarce, it was trucked in. Whenever battles were fought far from water supplies, the men often surrendered to inferior troops just for a cup of it. Gasoline was also scarce, and often had to be transported long distances over sandy tracks along with the water.

Although the Bolivians had state-of-the-art equipment purchased from Germany, it was unsuited for the Chaco. The huge armored tanks were unable to pass through the scrub and thorn bush, so men had to march ahead, swathing paths in 38°C (100°F) temperatures. (Tanks usually precede infantry.) The tanks had to leave every hatch open because of the heat, thus making them ideal targets for enemy grenade practice. Even with their inferior equipment, the Paraguayans were better suited to the terrain.

By mid-1933 Paraguay had made great gains, pushing the Bolivians into the foothills. Kundt was sent back to Germany and General Enrique Peñaranda took over, albeit unsuccessfully. President Daniel Salamanca was called to the battlefront for a military inspection. Dying of stomach cancer, emaciated with parchment skin and yellowed eyes, he never saw his dream of controlling the waterways to the Atlantic realized. As the Bolivians retreated, General Peñaranda and Major Busch forced Salamanca to resign. They put José Luis Tejada Sorzano, a liberal, into the driver's seat.

Basically, the war went like this: the Bolivians attacked the Paraguayans in the jungle and the Bolivians died like flies of dysentery and malaria. The Paraguayans chased the Bolivians 480 kilometres (300 miles) into the foothills and the Paraguayans died of hypothermia and altitude sickness. After three long miserable years, the war tallied over 180,000 dead soldiers from both sides who had died mostly from disease and infection rather than gunshot wounds. A truce was signed in June 1935, although peace negotiations continued for three more years until a border was finally drawn. Paraguay took about three-quarters of the Chaco and Bolivia was given access to a port on the Atlantic. Bullet-riddled machines and sandbagged trenches can be seen in the Chaco museum in Villamontes, where visitors also get a feel for the excruciating heat in which indigenous men from the mountains—more accustomed to cool temperatures—were expected to fight. The ritual fight between men who live at 4,000 metres (12,000 feet) and men who live at 300 metres (1,000 feet) is re-enacted every year in soccer games between the two countries.

Post-Chaco, Pre-Revolution

The loss of the territory in the Chaco was humiliating and financially disastrous for Bolivia. The drop in tin prices during the Depression exacerbated the problem. Tejada had replaced Peñaranda and was quickly overthrown

MATERIAL
DESTRUIDO

During the Chaco War more men died from thirst than bullets, though this wasn't the case for the men in this truck.

by the totalitarian Colonel David Toro Ruilova, who was backed by Chaco War hero General Germán Busch. A new group of men, known as the Chaco Generation, were now in power, and they questioned Fascist leadership. Their left-leaning slogan became, "Land to the Indians, mines to the state!" Toro belonged to the National Socialist Party and followed the philosophy of "what was good for the military was good for the country."

He taxed the rich and used the money for social programs. He increased wages, formed the Banco Minero to promote small business, and reformed working conditions. His biggest contribution was that he expropriated Standard Oil and nationalized the oil reserves. But the world economic depression and the Chaco War debt soared inflation to 600 percent. Everyone was unhappy.

Toro was overthrown a year later by Busch, his one-time supporter. But Busch was paranoid, ambitious and brutal. Born in the isolated town of San Javier, a mission town near Santa Cruz, and then schooled in Trinidad in the Amazon, he'd never seen a city until he entered the military academy in his late teens. He became a ruthless leader during the Chaco War and aided in the overthrow of both presidents Daniel Salamanca and José Luis Tejada. But political balance eluded Busch and he oscillated between right- and left-wing philosophies. Once in power in July 1937 he changed the constitution and declared himself totalitarian dictator, which gave him free hand to suppress monopolies, but he also promoted women's suffrage and education for all. He decreed that mine owners were to turn over their foreign earnings in exchange for worthless *bolivianos*.

Busch remained in power for two years, implementing reform until he was "encouraged" to commit suicide in 1939. His expropriation of Standard Oil never came to be, and neither did his decree to take foreign earnings from the Tin Trinity.

Prelude to Revolution

The miners' new power was represented in their political parties, and augmented by World War II when tin demand went up. Even though there were uprisings, coups, corrupt elections and a few responsive governments who tried to help, there was never any noticeable change for the Indians. But now sympathy for the mostly Indian working class was spreading, and land reform was talked about virtually everywhere, from the legislature to the simplest hovel. Then the talking transformed itself into action.

Just before the 1944 new year, the streets of La Paz were jammed with traffic cops stopping the few private vehicles that were moving along the Prada and forcing the drivers to the police station. It was about an hour after midnight. By early morning, the radio stations announced that a takeover by the National Revolutionary Movement (MNR) had been successful. Although some people rejoiced over their morning coffees, it was a nervous celebration. They could hear shots being fired, with the most noise coming from the army barracks. It seemed like the police were fighting the army, when they'd always been allies.

After the police seized the army barracks, the citizens felt safe enough to scream popular anti-American, anti-Semitic, and anti-Tin Trinity slogans from their balconies. Some helped stone the US Embassy. The people watched police haul government leaders off to jail, including President Peñoranda. A known fascist, Peñoranda was a supporter of the tin barons and a supporter of US President Roosevelt's Good Neighbor policy, a plan that offered tons of money in the way of low-interest loans to Latin countries willing to pledge allegiance to the Allies rather than the Axis countries. Like Peron in Argentina, Peñoranda preferred Mussolini but knew better than to go against the US, especially when Roosevelt was offering money in exchange for loyalty.

Behind the scenes, Victor Aramayo escaped incarceration by taking sanctuary in the Spanish Embassy. Patiño refused to speak to anyone from the safety of New York. Hochschild ran off to Chile and left his holdings in the hands of trusted employees. Those with nerve entered the streets and looted, vandalized and destroyed. Plaza Murillo was once again lit aflame. The US newspaper reported that the Good Neighbor policy had fallen apart.

As things cooled, the MNR announced the new cabinet. Major Gualberto Villaroel, a young, light-skinned Chaco War hero, became president. He believed in a military-social society that recognized unions and social rights such as the right to retire with pension (though pensions weren't implemented for another half a century). His vice-president was the popular Dr. Victor Paz Estenssoro, who was the same age, 35, as Villaroel. Paz Estenssoro was known for his charismatic and intellectual diction. He'd been arrested two years previous for allegedly plotting a coup. This was never proven; the real problem causing discomfort in the Peñoranda government was Paz Estenssoro's sympathies with the working class. Paz Estenssoro was affectionately called "El Jefe"—the boss—by his mates, and "the brains" by journalists worldwide. The other two notable characters in the lineup were Carlos Montenegro, described by journalists as an extreme Fascist, and Major Alberto Taborga, head of the police. Since Taborga controlled the men carrying most of the guns, he was the most powerful man in government. But the new leaders were subscribing to what is now commonly called "Peronist" politics—a mix of fascism and socialism that made the US nervous.

It was in this atmosphere that the citizens of Bolivia took a cautious look at their new government. Under the urging of Juan Peron, Argentinean president Edelmiro Farrell sent praise to Bolivia through its government-controlled newspaper. The biggest mistake the MNR made was resorting to violent tactics in dealing with the right-wing, pro-capitalist opposition. They shot most dissidents and, much to the ire of the general public, threw the bodies over a 900-metre (3,000 foot) cliff.

A Mexican politician once expressed amazement that the US could understand itself so well, but no one else. Paranoia about socialism and communism made the US back any political force that protected business, and it was easier to deal with a dictator than a politician who depended on the people's goodwill to get elected. By mid-July 1946 Villaroel was overthrown, and his body was hung from a lamppost in Plaza Murillo. Paz Estenssoro fled to Argentina. After the war, tin prices crashed taking the fire out from under the miners' unions. Most of the miners moved on to the country's biggest industry at the time—coca production for sale to Colombian drug cartels. This industry was run, for the most part, by the La Paz oligarchy. The generals bought up land and hired unemployed miners to work it. There were no unions on the coca plantations.

II

THE 1952 REVOLUTION

For the majority of Bolivians, the 1952 revolution is probably the most important historical event since independence.

A number of interim and provisional presidents and military juntas followed the collapse of the MNR in 1946. They reversed all social reforms and outlawed the MNR. By 1951, discontent was rampant throughout the country. The economy continued to decline due to depleting mineral resources and plunging prices. Ninety percent of agricultural land was owned mostly by the rich whites who were farming coca, and they didn't give the poor much for their own bellies.

With the help of public pressure, the MNR—with Paz Estenssoro now back in the country and serving as leader—won the right to run candidates during the 1951 elections. The MNR won with a large majority. But the right-wing groups annulled the elections, in part because the MNR was technically an illegal party. The outgoing president resigned and was replaced by a 10-man military junta of which he was a member. The MNR went back underground and Paz Estenssoro worked out of Argentina.

Demoralized, the middle class, the peasant workers and most of the military joined together in January 1952 in a huge hunger march that gave the absentee leaders of the MNR a sense of support. Paz Estenssoro plotted an overthrow with General Antonio Seleme, a member of the junta who was in control of the national police, and General Rene Barrientos, who was in charge of the air force.

On April 9, 1952, the MNR seized arsenals and gave arms to civilians, many of whom were miners. They blocked troops on their way to protect La Paz. After three days of fighting, the junta deserted the country and the army surrendered. Depending on the source, between 450 and 600 lives were lost. On April 16, Paz Estenssoro became president in recognition of his 1951 election success. It was Bolivia's 179th revolution since independence, and the most significant in its history because it involved such a wide range of people, and because it gave the Indians civil and political rights that would prove difficult to take away.

After the battle, General Barrientos flew to Argentina to escort Paz Estenssoro back to Bolivia, and MNR supporters marched up the hill to El Alto airport to welcome him. A little later, 50,000 people amassed in the Plaza Murillo to listen to his speech. "I was not lucky enough to be with you in your heroic hour, but now my life is yours!" he declared. "We shall study nationalization of the mines." The crowds roared.

The dead were buried and the wounded cared for with Argentinean medical supplies that arrived in trucks painted with photos of Juan and Eva Peron. Paz Estenssoro disarmed the 10,000 civilian troops who had been supplied with rifles, machine guns and ammunition, and reorganized them so only the most loyal were armed. Before getting their guns, they were required to swear allegiance to the revolution.

Victor Paz Estenssoro

Once the chaos settled, Paz Estenssoro started making the changes his party had promised before the revolution. The mines, which were 72 percent foreign-controlled and the source of almost all foreign exchange, were nationalized. Supervised by Marxist labor leader Juan Lechin and the Central Worker's Union (COB), the workers ran the companies. Under international pressure, the government paid the mining barons US$27 million for their holdings. Even though international tin prices were in free fall and it wouldn't matter who operated the mines, they were doomed to close and were not worth the money the MNR paid for them, but the word was the government had to pay or face an international boycott. The price broke the government and made Paz Estenssoro's followers unhappy.

Land was taken away from the large landowners and redistributed. Universal suffrage was expanded to include illiterates, the indigenous population, and those without property, resulting in the voting list rising from 200,000 to almost a million. Education was made available for the poor, medical clinics were established and cooperatives were set up so profits could go to the producers. The government developed roads, built hydroelectric dams, and financed sugar mills and cotton production.

This all sounds good, but economically, the country had fallen apart. There was no revenue from the nationalized mines, the social programs were costing, and the redistributed land wasn't yet in full production. Paz Estenssoro printed money to bankroll his debts, causing inflation to rise to 900 percent. Protests and rebellions increased.

The US moved in with a rescue plan. In November 1953, American Senator Homer Capehart, chairman of the Senate Banking Committee, came waving cash to aid the poor under the International Monetary Fund (IMF) banner. But another rebellion was taking place, this time in Cochabamba. Capehart and Paz Estenssoro met and negotiated between the interruptions of battle reports. Armed pro-government men stopped the rebellion, the sixth since Paz Estenssoro had come to power. This rebellion saw 23 dead, the closure of two anti-government newspapers, and hundreds of rebels jailed.

The IMF agreement required Bolivia to stop wage increases and food subsidies, balance its budget and create a single exchange rate. Within a year, the country stabilized and foreign investment money started to flow in.

Paz Estenssoro then reorganized the MNR so it resembled Mexico's popular party, Partido Revolucionario Institucion. But according to the term limits outlined in the constitution, Paz Estenssoro wasn't allowed to run in the 1956 election. So Hernan Siles, MNR founder and lifetime friend of Paz Estenssoro—but with a centre-right, middle-class political philosophy rather than a Socialist-Peronist one—took power. Infighting and philosophical disharmony instigated by Marxist Juan Lechin resulted in Paz Estenssoro running again in the 1960 elections. But he had the unpleasant job of disarming the miners living in the country. These men, unlike those living in or near La Paz, had kept their weapons since the 1952 revolution. Lechin disapproved and demanded more reforms. Gradually Estenssoro and the MNR became more conservative and antagonistic to the unions. The army was rebuilt and the communist party was suppressed. Paz Estenssoro amended the constitution and permitted his own re-election in 1964 with General Rene Barrientos as vice-president.

By the end of the year, a violent military junta led by General Barrientos ended the revolution and put the country back into the hands of the military. But land reform held and the broadening of the electoral base brought the Indian population—who now controlled agriculture—into mainstream politics.

From Barrientos to Banzer

General Rene Barrientos had been the most popular MNR leader in the fragmenting Paz Estenssoro administration. Barrientos was debonair, charismatic, and known for feats of valour. The 1964 coup that partnered Barrientos with General Alfredo Ovando sent Paz Estenssoro and Lechin, who had by now broken from the MNR, into exile. Barrientos held an election in 1966, which he easily won as leader of the small Christian Democrat Party.

Barrientos was against organized labour unless he controlled it, and he was especially against miners. He accepted military aid from the US to help combat communism, which made him very popular in Washington. He was winding down the revolution.

But then things started going wrong for the tough guy. His soldiers killed 30 striking miners in San Juan. They also executed Che Guevara, even though the Americans wanted him alive. Barrientos had wanted to see Che's head on a spike in downtown La Paz, not buried under an airstrip. The miners became even more militant. To add to Barrientos's woes after the capture and death of Guevara, Antonio Arguedas, minister of the interior, escaped to Havana with Che's diary. From Cuba, Arguedas declared himself a Marxist and revealed that many of Barrientos's aides were on the CIA payroll.

Barrientos died in a plane crash in April 1969 while trying to regain his popularity by visiting outlying villages. Many Bolivians thought the plane crash wasn't an accident.

Vice-president Luis Adolfo Siles Salinas, son of former president Siles Reyes (1926–1930) and member of the Christian Democrat Party, replaced Barrientos. Siles supported the mayor of La Paz, who was often in conflict with the commander of the armed forces, General Alfredo Ovando. Siles remained in power for only five months before he was overthrown by Ovando, but Ovando had expected to win the upcoming 1970 elections anyway.

The Arguedas scandal had given Ovando reason to split from Barrientos. Left was in vogue; Peru had Juan Velasco and Panama had Omar Torrijos. Ovando, a staunch MNR supporter, set his chessboard by favouring changes in living conditions for the poor and nationalizing Gulf Oil Corp. He awarded leftist intellectuals seats in his cabinet. Bolivia became polarized. The oligarchy and military brass teamed up. A bloody coup—this time led by General Miranda—on October 6, 1970, forced Ovando to flee. He'd been in power 14 months. Much of the country didn't support Miranda and violent protests flared up throughout Bolivia. General Juan José Torres emerged as the moderate compromise with just the slightest left leanings. His presidency lasted 11 months, a long time for this climate. All Torres did was put out political fires.

Finally, in August 1971 another coup, instigated in Santa Cruz and led by Colonel Hugo Banzer Suarez, resulted in Banzer slamming his butt into the leader's seat while Torres fled to Argentina, where he would be murdered five years later by right-wing death squads. With American and Brazilian support the "communist" witch-hunt in Bolivia became violent and severe. Banzer closed the universities, banned all left-leaning political parties, sent foreign priests and nuns packing and suspended the MNR-supported Central Obrera Boliviana (COB), a trade union federation formed after the 1952 revolution and led by Lechin. Banzer took control of the military and dispelled any hope of a future election. It was made clear throughout the country that no opposition to him would be tolerated. The Banzerato period, as it was called, brought peace to the middle class, but the foreign loans the new government received and pocketed threw Bolivia's debt beyond record levels.

When Banzer became dictator, the Nixon administration was in power in the US. Nixon didn't want communism spreading to any country in the western world, so the two countries participated actively in Operation Condor. It was right up Banzer's alley: give me money and I will give you dead bodies. The military aid from the US during Banzer's first year of power was twice as much as the previous 12 years put together.

12

THE INTERLOPERS

The years of the revolution, from 1952 to 1964, were—ironically—the most politically stable in the history of Bolivia. But corruption, falling prices in tin and no foreign investments caused inflation and put an end to the stasis. Banzer's dictatorship made it clear that the old order had returned. Meanwhile, though, Bolivia had caught the attention of the world. It seemed that, in this small country, a real workers' and people's revolution had taken place, producing permanent effects in land reform and enfranchisement of the indigenous. That revolution had been homegrown, with no influence from mainstream communism or international capitalism. This activated outside elements that started to intrude on Bolivian life as the revolution drew to a close and dictatorship returned.

These outside influences were the CIA, international communism and globalism, and they are represented by three men: Klaus Barbie, Che Guevara and Jeffrey Sachs. The first to arrive was Klaus Barbie, the Nazi Butcher of Lyon.

Klaus Barbie (a.k.a. Altman)

During an interview in La Paz in 1974, while the "Butcher of Lyon" was enjoying upper-crust freedom, he arrogantly declared, "Of course I'm proud of what I did during the war. If it hadn't been for me, France would be a Soviet Socialist Republic by now." He was under the protection of the CIA because he had information he was willing to sell. The information focussed on Barbie's wartime activities of turning socialist and labour sympathizers in France and Germany over to Hitler. But Barbie also knew the names of 20 double agents who had survived the war and the CIA wanted them badly. Barbie traded this information for safe passage out of Austria along the "ratline," an underground railroad run by Dr. Krunoslav Draganovic, a Croatian priest. The ratline smuggled Nazi criminals into Italy where they obtained false documents before moving to Central and South America.

Klaus Barbie was born in 1913 in the village of Godesberg on the River Rhine in Germany. He was the illegitimate son of two Catholic teachers of French ancestry who'd had an affair and later married when Klaus was a few months old. Knowing his family had fled France during the reign of Louis XIV helped form Barbie's hostile sentiments toward the French.

His father was a ranting disciplinarian given to booze. Barbie, to his own relief, was sent away to middle school at age 10 only to have his parents move close to him two years later. He was again exposed to his father's tirades. Young Klaus was not a good student, but he had a natural gift for languages that would serve him well in later years. His father's discipline and the circumstances of his birth caused a severe inferiority complex—this would help produce the sadist Barbie eventually became.

Tragedy hit in 1933 when his father died of a tumour supposedly caused by an old World War I bullet wound. That same year, his brother died of a heart condition. The deaths plunged the family into financial difficulty and ruined Barbie's possibilities of a post-graduate university degree. His undergraduate marks were low anyhow, and after leaving school he couldn't find a job. He joined the Nazi Party within months of his father's and brother's deaths, and his future was decided. He was assigned a position at a work camp in Schleswig-Holstein and was so smitten with ideology that he became a fanatic. A year later he found himself in the German Resistance in the French-occupied Rhineland. His Nazi beliefs contributed to his personal vendetta against the French.

After passing the scrutiny of a racial purity test, Barbie became part of the Sicherheitsdienst Security Service, an elite intelligence division of the SS, and on his first assignment learned the skills of investigation and interrogation. Hitler and the Nazi Party felt that Berlin at that time was a dirty, depressed city overrun with thousands of prostitutes, homosexuals and petty criminals. Barbie's assignment was to purify Berlin by rounding up all the "undesirables." He did this by frequenting the gay bars and whorehouses. His success in arresting, torturing and imprisoning these "undesirables" gave him automatic membership to the Nazi elite and by 1938 he was selected to attend a leadership course. Barbie didn't like the intense physical training but managed to graduate and become a second lieutenant.

Britain declared war against Germany in 1939, shortly after Germany invaded Poland. In early 1940, Barbie went to La Hague and Amsterdam to solve the "Jewish problem." He earned a reputation for brutality and viciousness and was awarded his first Iron Cross for beating to death an ice cream vendor who didn't salute him correctly. He was again promoted for ratting out resistance cells and Jews in hiding.

By 1943, Barbie was head of the Gestapo in Lyon, France, a stronghold of the resistance fighters. The Nazis knew he wouldn't flinch at killing huge numbers of civilians and this was one place they felt the civilians needed controlling. Barbie's cruelty knew no bounds and earned him the title "Butcher of Lyon." He was known to pluck people off the street like feathers off a chicken and then take them to his headquarters at the morbidly named Hotel Terminus, where he personally tortured them until they either said something useful or he became bored. His biggest hit was the capture, torture and killing of resistance fighter Jean Moulin, for which he received another first class Iron Cross, this time personally awarded by Hitler. The capture and brutal death of Moulin is what gave Barbie the idea that he actually saved France from communism.

After the war, Barbie stole from the Reich offices a stack of files that contained names of Soviet agents and their methods of operation. He went into hiding in Bavaria under the protection and pay of the American Counterintelligence Corps, for whom he worked as an informant. In return he was offered protection from an extradition to France for war-crime trials. Barbie acquired inside information on American operations and methods of interrogation. When the French started mumbling about putting him on trial, the Americans thought it better he not "go public."

The CIA justified its employment of Barbie by the fact that they did not have sufficient intelligence operations in Europe with which to sniff out dangerous pre-war Communists who had gone underground. The Americans worried about the morality of protecting Nazi war criminals, but reasoned that hiring a spy with the same standards of character as those in the civil or military service of the US was unrealistic, and so they went against the very nature of counterintelligence.

When the French again demanded his arrest, Barbie travelled the ratline to South America. In 1957 he applied for citizenship in Bolivia, where 8,000 welcoming Germans—who had immigrated during Bolivia's friendly period with Prussia before and during the Chaco War—already lived. In the meantime, the French had tried and convicted him in absentia for his war crimes, but couldn't locate him for execution.

Barbie married a Bolivian woman, had Bolivian-born children and became a legal citizen. He spent many hours in the Confiteria—still a popular tourist restaurant in downtown La Paz—drinking sweet cream-thickened coffee, devising techniques with other torture specialists, and advising leaders on how to efficiently work intelligence services. When he saw a visiting German ambassador in a restaurant in 1966, Barbie gave him the Hitler salute. The ambassador ordered Barbie removed. As he was being escorted out, Barbie yelled, "Damned Ambassador! I was an officer in the Gestapo, and when the party rises again I will settle my accounts with you!"

In the early 1970s, Robert Wilson, a visiting tourist and writer from Vancouver (and an ex-convict, according to the CIA) claimed that Barbie told him that he'd been to the US three times, and even gave the dates. Wilson also told the CIA that he was Barbie's biographer. In 1983, when the US was facing accusations of assisting war criminals, Wilson broke the Barbie-in-the-US story to the *New York Times*. It was later confirmed that Barbie did, in fact, enter under diplomatic status and took his young son Klaus George with him. While there Barbie also took a one-day trip from Florida to the Bahamas but, of course, was never detected.

As time passed, more Nazi criminals were brought to court. France wanted Barbie for the death and torture of 26,000 people, and particularly for the death of Moulin. In 1971 Serge and Beatte Klarsfeld, two Holocaust survivors and Nazi hunters, identified Barbie in La Paz, but the Bolivian government didn't have an extradition agreement with France. In January 1972 the news that Bolivia was harbouring a Nazi war criminal hit the papers. By May Barbie had admitted he was in fact Klaus Barbie, alias Altman, and that he worked for the German SS during the war. But he did not admit being head of the Gestapo in Lyon. In April 1973 the Bolivian government put Barbie in jail in La Paz while the courts decided whether he could be extradited. They asked the French for compensation if they turned him over. At the time, Barbie could be extradited to Peru and from there sent to France. Peru was in agreement but Georges Pompidou, the premier of France, refused to pay what Bolivia demanded, so Barbie went free.

During this period of freedom, Barbie acted as consultant to Luis Garcia Meza, a right-wing military general who gained power during the 1980 Cocaine Coup (see Chapter 14) that resulted in two years of repressive rule for Bolivians and freedom for drug lords. Barbie was also made president of the Bolivian State Navigation Society, an honourary position that provided a government paycheque.

It wasn't until 1983 that he was extradited to France in exchange for a cargo plane full of weapons, US$50 million, and a boatload of wheat. Now another problem arose. Although he'd received the death sentence during his 1952–54 trial in absentia, France had a 20-year statute of limitations that had long since passed. They adjusted their indictment to charge him with crimes against humanity, first introduced in the Nuremburg trials, which had no time limit attached. In Barbie's case they used this law to hold him responsible for the death of 44 children from Izieu Jewish Children's Home who had been sent to the Auschwitz concentration camp. The prosecutors had a signed telegram showing that Barbie was acting of his own volition rather than just following orders when he sent the children to their death.

Arrogant to the end, Barbie requested to be absent from court during the trial because, he argued, he was a Bolivian citizen deported illegally to face a lynching campaign started by the French media. Barbie was tried in absentia as he rested comfortably in his French jail cell. He was sentenced to life in prison, where he died of cancer four years later.

Che Guevara

Born in 1928 in Argentina, Ernesto Guevara was plagued with debilitating asthma. Unable to participate in many children's games, he instead read from his father's collections of Marx, Engels and Freud, although he admitted years later to his wife that he understood little of *Das Kapital*. As a university student Ernesto became anti-Peron even though he never participated in demonstrations calling for Peron's fall.

A bit unkempt, he was often heard boasting that he hadn't bathed for 25 days or that he had started wearing long pants because his shorts were so dirty they had to be thrown away. This earned him the nickname "Chancho" (pig). He also liked to shock, and thus earned the name "El Loco" (crazy). In South American Spanish, "*che*" is the equivalent of "hey," used similarly to the English Canadian "eh."

Guevara studied medicine, specializing in dermatology in general and leprosy in particular. But he was restless and had socialist ideals, so in 1949 he left on his famous motorbike trip north. Along the way he worked at everything from ditch digging to doctoring in specialized clinics for leprosy. He passed through Bolivia during this first trip.

In a subsequent journey, Guevara arrived in Bolivia via the US to become part of the 1952 revolution. But he found it an opportunists' revolution—not pure enough—and refused to participate. Instead, he went to Guatemala where he earned a living writing travel articles. He became an even purer socialist, rejecting all but the most unadulterated forms of communism (though he later admitted he didn't really understand what he was rejecting or accepting and Marx's analyses were too complicated for him). He lived with, and later married, Hilda Gadea, an Indian and Marxist who influenced Che's ideas.

Che met Raul and Fidel Castro in Mexico City in 1954 and followed them to Cuba, where Che studied and then practised guerrilla warfare. He became ruthless, shooting without question those he suspected of being traitorous, no matter from which side. He hated a turncoat. He also hated cowards and shot even those just suspected of cowardly acts. With this type of dedication it didn't take long for Che to become Fidel's top man. After persuasion from Che, Fidel finally agreed that anyone who deserted, showed insubordination or displayed defeatism would be shot. When Che heard of a deserter from the Cuban National Army who was tortured, shot and hung, he claimed the incident was sad but instructive.

After the revolution was won, Che was sent to the United Nations in New York where, as Minister of Finance representing the new Cuban government, he gave a famous speech about the rise of socialism and the death of Western imperialism. He voted for the Chinese to become members of the UN and for nuclear disarmament, starting with the US. This speech dispelled any hopes for financial aid from the Americans.

Once back in Cuba, Che disagreed with Castro, who was succumbing to Soviet pressure to accept Soviet policies rather than follow Che's purist ones. Restless for more revolution, he used this disagreement as an excuse to leave Cuba.

Che and his second wife, Olidia—whom he married one month after divorcing Hilda in May 1959—visited the African Congo, but he felt Africans weren't ready for revolution. He returned to Bolivia believing that the country, because of its poverty, was ripe for insurrection. Bolivia also bordered five countries, so Che felt that the spread of his revolution, once won in Bolivia, would be easy.

Using a fake name and passport, and with an army of about 75 men, Che crossed into Bolivia on November 4, 1966. By now the Bolivian revolution was over, Paz Estenssoro was in exile and the charismatic Barrientos, who had helped Paz Estenssoro take over in 1952, was fighting the unions. Che failed to see the importance of this. Instead of joining the miners and gaining their confidence, he formed a guerrilla training camp in Santa Cruz that attracted almost no support from locals who were known to resent any foreign interference in their politics. Che also disagreed with the Bolivian Communist Party's secretary Mario Monje about the guerilla expedition. He was a typical interloper with no sense of the country he was trying to liberate.

In February 1967, Che and his men left Santa Cruz and moved south and west, to Ñancahuazu, 20 kilometres north of the present town of Camiri and toward the highlands, where they set up camp. By the end of March the men were getting nervous. Food was running short and spotter planes buzzed overhead, trying to locate their camp. They decided to head farther into the foothills, toward Samaipata. With little food and water, they hacked their way through the spiny underbrush in the blazing heat of day, which would be replaced by the numbing cold winds and rain at night. Unable to obtain food from the terrified locals, the ragtag group ate their animals. Che's asthma made him so emaciated and weak that he had to be carried on a hammock. But in mid-April they successfully ambushed Bolivian troops, killing seven and injuring four, which raised their spirits.

On July 6, six of the men entered the hospital at Samaipata, a traveller's resting station and home of the pre-Inca ruin El Fuerte. They exchanged fire with soldiers at the garrison, took 10 hostages and purchased medicine at the pharmacy for Che. Just out of town, they stripped the hostages of their clothes and left them at the side of the road. The medicines proved useless in alleviating Che's asthma.

On June 14, suffering severely, Che celebrated his 39th birthday by recording in his diary a premonition that his days as a revolutionary were numbered.

On June 26 the group was caught in a crossfire and Che's longtime friend, Carlos Tuma Coello, was shot in the stomach and died in Che's arms. "I lost an inseparable companion of many years . . . whose absence I already feel like that of a son," Che wrote. Then on July 30, fellow revolutionary José Maria Martinez Tamayo, whom everyone called "Papi," was killed during a surprise attack. By the end of July, Che's forces were reduced to 22, with two of those injured.

Unbeknownst to Che, the US, still smarting about the Cubans and the Bay of Pigs fiasco, was tracking him. CIA agent Felix Rodriguez arrived in Bolivia on August 1, 1967, and worked closely with the Bolivian Army in the manhunt. Once in the vicinity of Guevara's group, the army first garnered support from the locals. They dropped pamphlets from the air saying they would pay US$4,200 for the capture of Guevara. Rodriguez then led a 650-man battalion into the area near Vallegrande. The people were forced to listen to megaphones blaring anti-guerrilla propaganda, leftists turned in by local informers were arrested, foreigners were questioned and the population "mobilized in the face of a possible Red attack."

By mid-August, Che split his band into two groups. He thought that the other group, led by Juan Vitalio Acuna Nuñez—a.k.a. Joaquin—was north of the Rio Grande, but heard on the radio that they were actually in the south travelling north. Puzzled, Che headed south to meet Joaquin. By now, Argentina and Peru radio stations were carrying reports of the skirmishes. During an early morning announcement it was reported that one of Joaquin's men had been captured by the military, tortured, and forced to reveal the rebels' whereabouts. As Joaquin's men headed north up the river, they were ambushed by the Bolivian army. All were massacred except for José Castillo Chávez (or Paco, as he was called), who escaped temporarily but was soon captured and taken to Vallegrande, where the dead bloated bodies of his comrades were on display in the laundry house of the Nuestro Señor de Mala Hospital. (When tourists follow the trail of Che today, one of the stops is the hospital.) Paco was marched back and forth like an organ grinder's monkey. Under CIA agent Rodriguez's persuasive encouragement, Paco— sick, bedraggled, and starved—began to talk.

By September 6, Che knew that Joaquin's group was gone, so he changed direction and headed toward the mountains. By the 21st, with some of his men so sick they were hallucinating, Che entered the village of Alto Seco to buy food and spend the night. But the mayor had heard of their impending arrival and informed the military. Che and his men took food from the mayor's store and spent the night talking revolution to the few peasants who would listen. The following day they went on to Loma Larga, a ranch between Alto Seco and La Higuera. The peasants living in Loma Larga fled.

Che continued on to La Higuera, but found that the men had abandoned the village, leaving only women and children. Seven of Che's men left to scout out the road toward Jaguey but were ambushed. Three died, two deserted and two returned, injured.

Shots were heard and Che surmised that the Bolivian military was hot on his tail, so he and his men moved toward Valle Serrano, south of the Rio Grande toward Paraguay, where he thought he'd find refuge. However, he was soon surrounded in a tiny forest above a canyon. On September 30, while the military celebrated their success entrapping the rebels, Che and his men snuck down to the river. After following the river for a week, they arrived at a steep ravine near La Higuera where a narrow passage led to the Rio Grande. It looked like they might slip through.

At noon, an old lady passed by. Che paid her fifty Bolivian pesos and warned her to keep quiet. Records show that it was an old woman who told the military that she heard voices of men on the Yuro River near San Antonio, and it is supposed that it was the same woman. The military took their positions above the camp of the revolutionaries.

The final battle started. It was October 8, 1967. Early in the fight, Che's M-2 carbine was hit in the barrel by a bullet. The next shot pierced his leg and a third hit his hat. As he retreated with his Bolivian comrade, Willy, he was hit several more times. Willy picked him up and ran. Che lost his hat. Willy sat down in an open plateau and tried to defend Che, but Willy was also wounded. Finally Che identified himself and claimed that he was worth more alive than dead. He surrendered. The battle ended at 3:30 p.m.

Lieutenant Colonel Selich, who was in command of the Bolivian troops, flew to La Higuera, where Che had been carried on a stretcher and placed in the schoolhouse. Che lay in the dirt, arms and legs tied, hair matted, clothes torn, bullet wounds adding to his discomfort. His rapid rasping breath showed his agony. Beside him were the dead bodies of two comrades killed earlier.

The next day, October 9, Colonel Joaquin Zenteno Anaya and Captain Ramos (a.k.a. CIA agent Rodriguez) arrived by helicopter. Rodriguez took some photos of Che and of his diary. At 12:30 a radio message from President General Barrientos in La Paz ordered the elimination of Che by the mayor of the village. The mayor partly complied. Rather than doing it himself, he gave orders to have him killed.

Rodriguez knew the Pentagon wanted to talk with Che, but he couldn't stop the Bolivians. He warned the firing squad not to shoot him in the face. Rodriguez wanted it to look like Che had been killed in battle, and thus wouldn't be available for interrogation by the Pentagon. As Che stood facing the firing squad his last words were, "Know this now, you are killing a man."

The Che Guevara Monument in Santa Clara, Cuba, where his remains now lie after being removed from Bolivia.

An autopsy performed in Vallegrande two days later proved that he had been shot through the heart; his face remained handsome and undamaged.

After Che was dead, Rodriguez took his Rolex watch, stored the body in the laundry room of the hospital, and then told the newly arrived gang of reporters that Che was still alive. When journalists wanted proof, military men brought the body out, its eyes open, head propped. He looked alive. If he had died in battle as Rodriguez originally reported, Che should have been dead 24 hours before the time stated on his death certificate.

Rodriguez had Che's hands cut off and the rest of him buried in an unmarked grave under the airstrip at Vallegrande. As for the newspaper reports, everyone knows that journalists never get anything correct when the news is breaking.

My rendition of Che's death is what I can understand from released CIA documents. However, according to Jon Lee Anderson, author of *Che*, Rodriguez took photos of Che while he was still alive, and these were stored in the files of the CIA for years.

Every October, Bolivians visit the school where Che Guevara was killed. They celebrate his heroism on the anniversary of his death. They offer guided trips to the canyon where the final battle took place and they encourage visits to the schoolroom and museum where Che spent his last hours. The laundry room is open for view. Copies of photos taken during this event are for sale and, strangely, no one seems to be interested in Che's communist ideology. He gave his short life trying to fight the establishment, plus he was handsome—these are the important things. It is also why Che gets onto t-shirts and everyone forgets about men like his comrade Joaquin. Even the Castro brothers don't rank as high in fame.

In 1997 the Bolivian government, complying with a request from Cuba, exhumed Guevara's remains and sent them to Havana. Castro had a mausoleum/museum built in Santa Ana, near the heart of the fighting for the Cuban revolution. The mausoleum entombs 11 of the revolutionaries, plus Che. The gigantic plaza in honour of these men always seems empty, except for the eternal flame and a huge statue of Che.

Jeffrey Sachs

While some might know Jeffrey Sachs better today for his theories on ending poverty in Africa, Bolivians know him as a major—and controversial—force in the drama of their struggling economy. By the age of 29, Jeffrey Sachs was a full professor of economics at Harvard, which suggests he is a very smart man. In 1985, when he was barely into his thirties, he was asked to apply his economic "shock therapy" to Bolivia. His theories had not been tested elsewhere. He had never worked on a real-life economy before. He worked enthusiastically with various Bolivian governments, but mostly with Banzer, until 2002. During this time he also took on Poland and Russia.

After the 1952 revolution, coca had become Bolivia's main source of income. The oligarchy and army brass bought estates, and so did the miners who were heading back to the land from Oruro and Pulcamayo as the mines closed. The crop went mainly to Colombia for processing and export.

Sachs's treatment had one objective: to hook Bolivia into the international economy by bringing it in line with the World Bank and the International Monetary Fund (IMF), so that corporations would be free to operate and loans could safely be given to kick-start the economy. The IMF has 184 countries as members, with each having voting rights according to its dollar power. Because the US is so rich, it dominates the IMF.

What the IMF and the World Bank wanted had been prescribed in the Bretton Woods agreement of 1944: to prevent financial problems like those suffered after World War I and during the Great Depression. The IMF and

World Bank sought a world economic order with the World Bank financing large-scale reconstruction and the IMF issuing loans to stabilize international currency exchange rates and bridge temporary imbalances of payments to keep the system going. These two organizations were to oversee the economies of 44 allied nations and, ultimately, the defeated Axis countries. France in 1947 was the first financial benefactor with a US$25 million loan. As the years went on, the loans got bigger and the recipient countries less developed. Kenya received US$190 million in 1983 to help with droughts, and Asia received US$21 billion during its financial crisis in 1997–98.

The rules were fairly simple. To participate, troubled countries had to eliminate restrictions on foreign investment, lift tariffs, get rid of subsidies, abolish labour rights, reduce state spending and privatize state enterprises including municipal utilities. This, they say, was the short-term discomfort for the long-term gain.

But the discomfort fell mainly on the poor. Theoretically, with less social spending, more money is made available to repay loans. (In other words, if you don't take your kid to the dentist, you can pay your ever-increasing water bill.) If the therapy didn't result in increased economic activity, loans couldn't be paid, so the IMF lent the ailing countries more money to meet their payments.

In Mexico, where the government followed recommendations to the word, the economic adjustments left over 50 percent of the people in abject poverty. Mortality rates tripled due to nutritional deficiencies and unemployment and bankruptcies increased.

In Bolivia, Sachs advised Victor Paz Estenssoro (during his last reign from 1985–89), to issue the proclamation known as decree 21060 or NEP—the New Economic Policy. As soon as the announcement was made—with the consent of Banzer and the ADN party—Paz Estenssoro put the country in a state of emergency to counter any opposition that he knew would come from other governmental parties and the workers. He then broke unions and privatized water providers, mining companies, oil industries, telephone companies, railways and the national airline. Salaries were decreased, 30,000 miners were laid off and underemployment became the norm. Health benefits were reduced and some pensions eliminated.

Inflation ran at 24,000 percent annually (though some sources say "just" 16,000 percent). Sachs got the government to devalue the currency, abolish the minimum wage and all state spending except for the government and army. Inflation disappeared but the economy seized up. Between 1986 and 2001, loans made in the amount of US$350 million were supposed to stimulate growth.

But nothing much happened, except for mounting debt. The loan money went into the pockets of the white elite and the coffers of foreign companies that had bought up railways, telephone companies, hospitals and utilities. Services stopped. But, there was no inflation.

When the policies didn't work, Sachs became defensive. He said, "I always told the Bolivians that what you have here is a miserable, poor economy with hyperinflation; if you are brave, gutsy and do everything right, you will end up with a miserable, poor economy with no inflation." But what Bolivia ended up with was a dead economy. The railways purchased by American and Chilean multinationals in Bolivia stopped working. The terminals in some cities like Cochabamba turned into vast markets, the track beds into shanty-suburbs. Electrical services collapsed. The national airline stopped flying.

Economists now say that Sachs went wrong in assuming that what worked for established countries with rule of law would work in Africa, Latin America, Poland and Russia. It didn't. Where you have a huge gap between the elite and the poor, and habitual bestowing of favours and receiving of bribes, globalism doesn't work. And it doesn't work because wealthy countries don't play by their own rules. Both the US and European countries subsidize and protect their agricultural industries. Farm-based economies like Bolivia's are dead if they sign into free trade agreements with countries that protect their farmers. Recently the US has put up steep steel tariffs. The Argentine example weighs heavily enough on Bolivia; like Mexico, Argentina did everything right and crashed. In Russia, the mafia ran off with most government assets and ruined the economy (although now, under new administration, it is prospering).

Sachs couldn't admit that democratic reform and/or socialism were important to any solution. Look at China—a booming economy despite breaking all the rules. The state owns the banks and controls investments. It should be a mess, but presently China owns most of America's debt. Sachs also failed to adjust his shock therapy to individual cases. When he started working with Boris Yeltsin in Russia, he hit a brick wall because the Kremlin crooks were always one step ahead of his suggested policies. Sachs resigned after two years. Presently, he's shifting ground to sustainable development, working on increasing aid, controlling malaria and building infrastructure mainly in Africa with the United Nations Millennium Project. He is trying to have the debts that he acquired for poor countries cancelled. Most economists summarize Sachs in his earlier years as "dangerously naïve." And Sachs himself agrees—Bolivia was a huge "teacher" for him.

13

OPERATION CONDOR, OPERATION SILENCE

From the 1952 revolution until the mid-1980s, a campaign of right-wing, so-called "counter-terrorism" operations that eventually grew into Operation Condor sent a wave of deaths, torture and human rights violations throughout Latin America. It was this operation that contributed to the death of Che Guevara and granted the good life to Klaus Barbie.

It started in 1976 with a car bomb that killed Orlando Letelier, minister of Chile's Allende government, and General Carlos Prats, Allende's vice-president. After Letelier was killed, an Argentine officer cabled a message to Washington saying, "It was a wild condor operation carried out by those lunatics in Santiago." For 16 years the only hint the public had of Operation Condor was the deaths of the two famous leaders.

Details like this came out in 1992, when what came to be known as the "terror archives" were accidentally discovered by a Paraguayan judge looking for a political prisoner's file. The documents revealed that by the mid-1980s, about 50,000 people had been murdered, 30,000 had disappeared ("*desaparecidos*"), and 400,000 had been incarcerated, mostly in concentration camps. The archives revealed the major participating members to be the secret police of Argentina, Bolivia, Brazil, Chile, Paraguay and Uruguay. Key players such as Brigade General Jorge Videla of Argentina, Augusto

Pinochet of Chile and Alfredo Stroessner of Paraguay sent teams of "intelligence agents" throughout South America and further afield into France, Portugal, Spain, Italy and the US to sniff out—and snuff out—political opponents. Colombia, Peru and Venezuela also cooperated to varying degrees. Operation Condor was the best-kept secret in underground networking of the modern age.

We now know the operation had been formalized during the Conference of American Armies held in Caracas in September 1973, when General Breno Borges Fortes of Brazil suggested a friendly "exchange of information" in the international struggle against subversion, which was generally considered communist-inspired. The incentive was money, mostly courtesy of the US government—then caught up in the Cold War. With financial incentives dangling in front of them, the dictators and army generals who ran most Latin American countries were happy to comply.

The rules and methods of Condor were formally drawn up at the Inter American Reunion on Military Intelligence meeting held in Chile on November 25, 1975—Pinochet's 60th birthday. It was the best gift Pinochet, who became the leading force, would ever receive, and he used it well for the rest of his reign.

A flow chart was drawn showing responsibilities, methods of communication and secret codes. Consultations, exchanged through a communication centre in the Panama Canal Zone, revealed the "who's who" of supposed subversion, listed suspected guerilla groups, described torture methods, determined ideal destinations for death flights (dropping live or dead bodies into the mountains or the ocean), and laid out the best methods for abducting children from selected leftist families.

Meanwhile, former president Juan José Torres, in hiding in Argentina, was shot, as were Uruguayan ministers Hector Gutiérrez and Zelmar Michelini. Bolivians Edgardo Enriquez and Jorge Fuentes, leaders of Movimiento de la Izquierda Revolucionaria (Revolutionary Left Movement or MIR), simply disappeared. Opposition from Omar Torrijos—a Panamanian army officer and a de facto leader who was against the use of the canal as the organizations' communications centre—was eliminated when his plane crashed over the ocean. It has since been suggested that his death was encouraged by the US under the pretense that Torrijos was harbouring a drug cartel; the official statement is that his plane malfunctioned. Manuel Antonio Noriega replaced Torrijos. Operation Condor is also believed to be behind the 1976 bombing of Cubana Air Flight 455, which killed 73 people.

Under the leadership of Hugo Banzer, who had won a military coup in 1971, Bolivia played a part in the torture and illegal detention of over 2,000 dissidents, violating all human rights laws. Banzer insisted that the dissidents were Communists taking orders from Communist political leaders, and therefore had to be eliminated.

General Suarez Mason of Argentina later admitted signing 50 to 100 death warrants per day for a long period of time during Jorge Rafael Videla's dictatorship in Argentina. The leftist movements in Nicaragua and El Salvador were also brought down, though that took open warfare.

Immediately after basic directives were in place, the work progressed and Operation Condor members assisted in Bolivia's Cocaine Coup, so-named because the participants were also involved with the drug cartels. The Cocaine Coup brought General Luis Garcia Meza to power and gave both Stefano Delle Chiaie and Klaus Barbie steady employment.

Operation Silence

Although not much changed in the administration's lineup, Operation Silence replaced Operation Condor in the 1980s. The switch happened because even the powers in Washington were shocked by the brutality unleashed during Operation Condor. Those suspected of committing crimes against innocent people were encouraged by their leaders to go into exile. Any resistance was corrected by a bullet or a sudden disappearance. At the same time, reprisals against those exiled servants of US foreign policy were forbidden. Bolivian president Colonel Luis Arce Gomez, who was in power at the time, is quoted as saying, "Bolivians opposed to the new order [Operation Silence] should walk around with their written will under their arms."

Operation Silence is responsible for the murder of men like Bolivian congressman Marcelo Quiroga Santa Cruz, chief advocate for bringing General Hugo Banzer to trial for human rights violations committed during Operation Condor. Hundreds of women were imprisoned to keep them silent about the execution of their husbands and the disappearances of their children. Doctors who refused to lie on death certificates were especially targeted, put in prison, and usually tortured. Political opponents were incarcerated or exiled and the press was censored.

After the 1989 democratic elections, Jaime Paz Zamora took office and a blanket of stability settled over the nation. Some human rights violators were brought to trial. Operation Condor and Operation Silence were over, and "commie" hunting was replaced with drug hunting.

It should be noted that Mexico, Costa Rica, Canada, France, Spain, the UK and Sweden accepted Latin American political refugees during this period.

14

ECONOMIC WARFARE

Over the years, America has grown fond of referring to its various foreign and domestic policies as "wars." There was a "war on crime," a "war on terror," and so on. The biggest of these to hit Latin America was the "war on drugs," named and launched by Nixon in 1971.

Similarly, Bolivians like to designate their struggles with globalism as wars.

Coca Drug War

Bolivia is South America's second-largest grower of coca. The use of coca dates back to 3000 BC. It was called *hoja angrada* ("sacred leaf") by the Inca, and was used as a gift to the gods. Indigenous people living in the Andes have long used the plant for religious and medicinal purposes. Even today Indians are often seen burning coca leaves at shrines close to where loved ones were killed. Coca is also used to decrease hunger, cold or altitude sickness. Miners in particular use it while working underground as an antidote to cold and hunger, and travellers use it to help acclimate themselves to such high elevations.

The coca leaf has long been an issue for colonial authorities and for whites in power. One attack on the leaf's reputation began in 1947 when a Peruvian, Dr. Carlos Gutiérrez-Noriega, indicated that coca chewing caused Indians to have negative attitudes toward the "superior"—Spanish—culture. His lobbying resulted in United Nations experts condemning the plant as "noxious and [. . .] causing racial degeneration." Its immediate eradication was recommended, but no one followed through.

In 1975 Harvard University analyzed the coca leaf for nutritional value and found it high in calories, protein, carbohydrate and fiber. The plant also contains iron, calcium, phosphorus, and vitamins A, E and B. And an anthropologist at Indiana

Coca has religious and medicinal value. Eradicating coca helped the rise of Bolivia's new president, the *cocalero* Evo Morales.

University has suggested that chewing coca after dinner may help regulate glucose metabolism and enhance digestion of carbohydrates at high altitudes.

Cocaine, a recreational drug and derivative of coca, was first discovered and produced in 1855. By 1869 cocaine was widely used as an additive to wines. By the beginning of the 20th century the drug cocaine was marketed as a mild stimulant by companies such as Coca-Cola. Until 1903, Coca-Cola spiked their drinks with an estimated nine milligrams of cocaine per glass for flavouring, promoting it as a mild intoxicant and alcohol substitute. (Interesting that in Bolivia coca tea, made with the leaf, is the drink of choice rather than Coca-Cola.) After 1903, while cocaine was still legal, sniffing the powder became popular. At about the same time the medical profession started using it as a local anesthetic, especially in dentistry. Sigmund Freud was so enamored with the drug he gave it to his patients, and became addicted himself.

In 1912 the US reported 5,000 cocaine-related deaths. Members of the temperance movement felt cocaine addiction was contributing to moral degeneration, so they campaigned to stop recreational use. In 1914 the drug was banned in America for anything but medical purposes. But cocaine had caught on, and by the 1970s the US consumed anywhere from 270 to 400 metric tons per year. Bolivia became the second-largest producer of cocaine in the western world.

Bolivia's production of cocaine had grown to an estimated 70 metric tons per year by 1999, although Bolivia supplied Colombia with a lot more than that in raw product. Since the US couldn't seem to stop cocaine use at home, they attempted eradicating the drug at the source in the "War on Drugs."

But drug money is big money, and Bolivian politicians often used it to finance their needs. Garcia Meza, with the help of drug lord Roberto Suarez and torture specialist Klaus Barbie, was involved directly in the Cocaine Coup of 1980. Banzer had supported Meza and Suarez, and during the June elections the following year, he formed a coalition with Meza to take the presidency. Both men were involved in protecting the drug lords, some of whom were rumoured to be Banzer's relatives.

But there was also opposition to the drug cartels. In 1984, under the leadership of anti-drug president Hernán Siles Zuazo, the head of Bolivian narco-traffic control, Rafael Otazo, met with drug lord Roberto Suarez at his hideout in the Beni and was offered US$2 billion toward the national debt in exchange for permission to traffic freely. Considering Suarez's power in South America—he had a private army, a private police force, and powerful connections in Colombia—he assumed Otazo would, after thinking about it, agree to his terms. Instead, Otazo released to the public the names of all officials and cabinet ministers connected with the drug trade after a plane carrying 1,161 kilos of cocaine was intercepted at the La Paz airport. The scandal didn't decrease production or trade, but the opposition, claiming the president was part of the agreement to allow drug running, impeached Siles.

In 1998 the US stepped up its anti-drug pressures and designated US$246 million for eradication programs beyond their own borders. This included Mexico, Colombia, Peru and Bolivia. Bolivian farmers were to receive about US$2,000 each to grow replacement crops such as pineapples, bananas, coffee or oranges. But many *cocaleros* (farmers growing coca) are in the isolated Chapare region south of Cochabamba, where roads are bad and shipping costs high. Farmers needed a crop that sold for a good price, so high-yield coca continued to be the crop of choice. Opposition to eradication programs increased.

In 2000 the US and Bolivia agreed to a plan that included building three military bases with $6 million in American assistance money. The bases, located in Chapare, would permanently house 1,500 soldiers to fight the war on drugs. Again the people of Bolivia protested and the idea was dropped.

As production of cocaine increased, Bolivian soldiers were encouraged to step up their efforts. They did so with the same fervour they'd displayed hunting communists during Operation Condor. They confiscated or burned coca plants, stole food and molested women. Torture and unexplained disappearances again became the norm.

True to form, Bolivian officials weren't beyond corruption either; they often sold the confiscated coca leaves—slated for burning—to the drug lords, and kept the profits. As the street-drug problem in the US increased, the Drug Enforcement Agency worked harder. Resentment grew until the *cocaleros* joined forces and resisted the DEA. The stones-against-guns conflicts left hundreds of burned buses along the roadsides and caused just as many needless deaths.

The soldiers became more vigilant. They stopped all vehicles and searched for chemical precursors used in cocaine production, incarcerating anyone carrying such items. Tourists became accustomed to the army roadblocks and searches. The ongoing conflict and inconvenience resulted in a general dislike of gringos—no one likes the heavy-handed action of the DEA and the army, especially in the Trinidad, Santa Cruz and Cochabamba areas. The searches continue and no one is exempt.

To prevent total chaos, the government compromised by permitting 74,000 hectares in the Yungas to remain in coca production, with Villa Fatima market in La Paz as the only legal outlet. One of the justifications for this is that traditional farmers in the Yungas use natural fertilizers and harvest

the leaf without incurring the environmental damage that the chemical fertilizers, used in Chapare, cause. Each week, enough leaves pass through the
Villa Fatima market to make a ton of cocaine. But the only purchasers are
registered retailers who take the coca leaf to other areas of the country to sell
to chewers and tea drinkers.

Despite the new rules, the *cocaleros* throughout Bolivia have continued
to produce both leaves and cocaine. During the first three months of 2006,
339 illegal cocaine laboratories in the Chapare region were located and
closed. Bolivian courts are continually crammed full of drug dealers waiting
for trial, but it is mostly considered a minor offence and a majority of the accused are freed. In these cases I would suspect the bribe system works best.

For most Indians living in the Andes, as has been stated before, the use
of coca is traditional and necessary for cultural practices. For interested travellers, the leaf is purchased for pennies in any market, and the crops that are
openly grown throughout the cultivating regions of the Chapare and Yungas
are easily visible. Under President Evo Morales, who comes from an Indian
cocalero background, the practice of producing coca is permitted.

It's no surprise that drugs are easy to come by in Bolivia—but believe
me, it's not worth the high. Remember that Bolivian prisons do not adhere
to modern North American human rights codes. If incarcerated, you spend
years waiting for trial unless you can bribe a judge to hear your case. Bolivians follow Napoleonic code—you are presumed guilty until proven innocent. Prisoners must purchase their own cell, bed, bedding and clothes.
Those unable to pay are left to sleep in the open areas, vulnerable to attack
by fellow prisoners.

Water War

The Chacaltaya Glacier feeds La Paz most of its water. With global warming,
the glacier is receding at an alarming rate—some scientists claim it will be
gone by 2015. The Chapare region has always been dry. The Yungas, the section of land between the Chapare and the Altiplano, is in the rainforest belt,
where water isn't much of a problem. But for those selling goods in the markets, or for the rural farmers trying to sell their meager excesses of produce,
purchasing clean drinking water is a luxury. When a traveller gets off the bus

in El Alto and walks past some of the shacks inhabited by Bolivia's poorest, it is plain to see that clean drinking water isn't a priority. Although tourists, rich by any Bolivian standard, can readily purchase water anywhere in the country, locals can't spare the money to do the same.

In 1999, under pressure from the World Bank and the International Monetary Fund (IMF), Bolivia signed a lease over to Bechtel Corporation and to a consortium of British investors, including Abengoa, for control over water in Cochabamba District. These companies already had control of the water in La Paz and El Alto. (Bechtel is the same company that dammed the Three Gorges on the Yangtze River in China.) In exchange for granting Bechtel a monopoly on water, Bolivia was forgiven US$600 million in debt to the World Bank, the IMF, and the Inter American Development Bank. According to Jim Shultz, executive director of the Democracy Center, foreign investors spent less than US$20,000 of up-front capital for Cochabamba's water system.

The takeover meant that the citizens of Cochabamba had no choice but to purchase water now under control of the foreign investors. They were also forbidden to use water from natural springs or private wells. While the ink was still wet on the lease, the company doubled and then tripled the local water rates. For some customers, their monthly bill suddenly jumped from the equivalent of US$12 to $30, for others from $5 to $20, and they had to pay it or their water was shut off. What's more, houses without meters were charged a basic rate at a substantial increase to what they were already paying. When a Bolivian income is usually around US$100 a month or less, $20 for water is an astronomical amount. And it's especially outrageous if you consider that water for a Washington, DC, household costs about $17 per month, while salaries there are at least 30 times higher than Bolivian salaries.

After water prices went up, a city strike was called for mid-January 2000 and Cochabamba was shut down. Not a single vehicle moved in or out of the city. The poor and middle class citizens—accountants, university students, priests, mothers, journalists, shopkeepers and campesinos who walked from surrounding villages armed only with clubs and stones—participated in the march. Even old women made roadblocks out of rocks and branches.

The government requested 24 hours of peace for negotiation time, and when that time was over, the people assembled in the plaza for Hugo Banzer's answer. They were met with 1,000 armed military and police, there to "protect the good citizens of Cochabamba from the troublemakers." The demonstrators were subjected to tear gas, rubber bullets and beatings; one TV station showed an unarmed man being beaten with a club. In the end, 175 protesters were injured, including two young men who were blinded. The government agreed to a rate rollback and freeze until November.

More information was uncovered and revealed by the press, rallying the people and focusing "troublemaker" sentiments. A public survey was held and 90 percent demanded discontinuation of the Bechtel contract. Finally, on April 7, 2000, another general strike was called; roadblocks went up and people took to the streets. By the next day, villagers living in Cochabamba District and even some from El Alto and La Paz joined the city protestors. By the third day, with no response from the government, people became impatient. They surrounded the government buildings where negotiations were again taking place. The government responded by arresting 15 protesters, including Oscar Olivera, a political activist and associate of then-congressman Evo Morales. The following morning, the 15 protesters were released and the government announced it would cancel the agreement over the water rights.

However, by 10 a.m. on the day after the announcement, Banzer went back on what he'd promised, declared martial law, and restricted freedom of the press. Radio stations were closed and electrical power was cut. The mayor resigned. Police raided private homes in search of protest leaders. Soldiers occupied the city. A 17-year-old youngster was shot in the head and died. Thirty were injured. And still, protesters marched into the city from outlying areas, skirting the roadblocks now held by the military. Women collected and cooked food for the out-of-town demonstrators. Banzer threatened more aggressive measures, and then appointed army general Walter Cespides as governor. (Cespides was responsible for numerous deaths during his command when he led the drug wars in the Chapare region in 1998.)

On April 11, the International Water Company (Bechtel's front) released a statement saying they were willing to cancel the contract at a cost of

US$25 million to the Bolivian government. While the government officials were reading the statement, Bechtel employees were ridding their offices of financial records and computers, emptying bank accounts and avoiding the bill collectors who wanted $150,000 in unpaid debts.

An arbitration firm, the International Center for Settlement of Investment Related Disputes (ICSID) was hired to settle the final restitution. The Bolivian government complained that ICSID was biased in favour of the private companies because its chair was the president of the World Bank. The American Association of Jurists and the Europe Third-World Center became involved and decided that the sum asked for was unreasonable. The Association of Jurists recommended that the ICSID be rejected and that the government meet the needs of its citizens by granting Bolivians their basic human rights, including the right to affordable drinking water.

In 2003, 300 organizations from 43 countries sent a Citizen's Petition to ICSID. The petition demanded the hearings be opened to the public and recommended that the companies drop the charges. In 2005 the ICSID ruled that the hearing should be public, but in January 2006 company representatives travelled to Bolivia and received a payment of two *bolivianos* (about 30 cents) as a token payment for their initial investment. This was the first time an international corporation working in Bolivia had dropped its fight as a direct result of public pressure. Reasonably priced clean water is just one of the benefits realized by this struggle. Every person, rich or poor, rural or urban, in Bolivia will tell you about his participation in the water war. All you have to do is buy the *chicha*.

Tax War

I was in Sorata looking down at the Mapiri Trail when the Tax Riots of February 2003—known as Febrero Negro, or Black February—broke out. The police were on strike to protest the new tax laws the government was trying to implement under the direction of the World Bank. The police stormed the government building while parliament was in session. The military was on guard, and someone fired a gun. Someone else fired back, and three days later 33 were dead and hundreds injured. Even President Sanchez de Lozada's chair held a souvenir bullet that had just missed his shoulder. As a *gringa* who speaks acceptable Spanish, I was able to cajole, joke and pay my way through the subsequent roadblocks and out of the country, although it did take a few days.

What happened was that the IMF had wanted the blacklisted Bolivian government to improve its credit rating by making interest payments on its loans. Had the government succumbed to the international investors during the Water War and ardently shot up protestors, these debts may have been reduced, but the government didn't—so the pressure was on. The IMF suggested an income tax. Economists declared that if the government taxed those earning twice the Bolivian minimum wage—which amounts to US$110 per month—the government's income would rise to US$80 or $90 million per year, most of which could go to repay the debt.

Only about one million Bolivians earn wages, and most of these are civil servants. Unfortunately, the police are a big part of the civil service and they were already riled because they hadn't received their January salaries and they'd been refused their salary increase demands. The government, while in negotiations with the IMF and World Bank, said over and over again that an income tax would cause social problems and that there would be resistance. The IMF and World Bank continued to insist, and the government gave in.

On February 11, 2003, the police asked for a meeting with the Minister of Government, Alberto Gasser. He refused, saying the tax proposal was non-negotiable. However, the following morning, Gasser entered talks at police headquarters—located across the plaza from the presidential palace and National Congress. He was met by a fully armed police force asking for 30 non-negotiable demands, including that the proposed tax only pertain to those making 5,000 *bolivianos* (US$660) per month or more. The answer was, *"No se puede."* It can't be done.

At ten o'clock, inspired by opposition leader Evo Morales—who had finished just two points behind President Sanchez de Lozada, a.k.a "Goni," in the elections—and led by the police, the people went on strike and marched toward the legislature. Youngsters from the nearby high school threw rocks at the presidential palace to the cheers of the police. The army standing guard at the palace responded with tear gas. The students ran toward the police station, where the police fired tear gas back at the military.

The military circled the plaza armed with rocket launchers, rifles and assault weapons. They fired rubber bullets and hit a police officer. A gun was fired and a shootout followed, with the police finally being driven out of the plaza.

Of the 33 casualties, most were civilians, and 182 people caught in the crossfire had been seriously wounded. In the final tally, the youngest of the dead was 11 and the oldest was 86. One sad story was of a handyman who climbed onto the roof of a building to collect the tools he had hastily left behind the previous day. A sharpshooter fired from across the plaza, killing him and a student nurse who went to help him.

The president announced the cancellation of the tax within hours. But once locals realized that the police were out of commission, they began vandalizing and stealing from the shops and unprotected bank machines. They also tried to destroy as many government records as possible, especially the records of those with pending trials.

The following day saw more riots in El Alto, Santa Cruz, Cochabamba

The three-day Tax War erupted when the government tried to legislate income tax. The rioters burned out the Ministry of Growth and Development in La Paz.

and Oruro. Protestors stormed the Coca-Cola bottling plant in El Alto and were fired upon by military helicopters.

I returned to La Paz a few days after the riots and saw a lot of damage to the buildings around the plaza. Numerous bank machines were torn apart. Two colonial buildings were burned out and the Vice-Presidential building was badly damaged. On the Prada, the Minesterio Desarrollo (the ministry of growth and development, where government records were kept) was gutted and still had black smoke belching from its windows. Today there are no physical traces of that altercation aside from a few pockmarked buildings.

The IMF officials in Bolivia at the time were able to escape out the back door. They offered their sympathies from Washington, and stated that they were still interested in negotiating with Bolivia.

Gas War

During his first term as president, Goni awarded contracts to 26 foreign petroleum companies without the approval of congress. Some of these included contracts with multinational gas companies for exploration and production, and this exploration was to be paid for by Bolivian gas consumers through gas price hikes. When the announcement was made in 1993, protests started. People not only hated the hikes but they also hated the fact that the raw gas was to be shipped through territory lost to their arch-enemy, Chile. According to international polling group Apoyo, the contracts were against the wishes of 81 percent of the population. The majority of Bolivians were in support of Morales and his opposition to gas increases.

During the next 10 years—as gas prices rose—organizations such as the Coalition for Defense of Gas, the Movement of the Landless, and the Peasant's Union sprouted like coca leaves. Roadblocks sprung out of the ditches and on some occasions, as many as 100,000 people took to the streets protesting both the gas prices and the coca drug war.

In Sorata in August 2003, the military went to rescue hundreds of people stuck on buses behind a roadblock put up in protest of the increasing gas prices. As the military headed for the roadblock, a tentative agreement was reached between the government and the campesinos. But when the military actually arrived, fighting broke out and went on until seven campesinos and two soldiers were dead. Twenty-five people were injured. In retaliation, the campesinos burned the oldest hotel in town—built in 1830 as a supply depot for those on the quinine, gold and rubber trade route—that had been a popular tourist accommodation filled with antiques. The military denied accusations of undue aggression but were discredited later by Bolivia's Congressional Human Rights Commission. The US arrived before the end of the month and gave $63 million in aid, but they concluded that the military intervention was justified.

Concerned Bolivian leaders called a strategic meeting in Cochabamba. Attendees included leaders from Movement toward Socialism (or MAS, Evo Morales's party), from People's High Command (this was Olivera of water-war fame) and from the Bolivian Workers Union.

Meanwhile, in La Paz, truck drivers demanded a price freeze on fuel, and the government agreed until pressure from the oil companies caused them to rescind. Goni, then on his second stint as president, offered to subsidize the loss of profits to the tune of US$7 million even though the companies already purchased the crude for 12 times less than international prices.

Roadblocks caused supplies in the city to diminish. On October 12, 2003, protestors blockaded the military and the police escorting gas trucks

Protest against American interference with Bolivian gas production.

into La Paz. The soldiers and police, already jumpy, opened fire at the protesters and the surrounding homes. Some protesters fought back with sticks and others fired slingshots. At the end of the day, 20 people lay dead; some were children. The following day more protests and confrontations left another 30 dead.

Strikes and roadblocks on October 17 finally brought La Paz to a standstill. The army and police killed 60 people while trying to suppress the opposition, and Goni was forced from office. He fled to Miami and currently lives quietly in Chevy Chase, Maryland. He is reputed to have pocketed much of the money paid to Bolivia for exploration leases. In 2005, Goni was served a summons from Morales's government to stand trial for the killings during the Gas War. To date, the summons has been ignored by both Goni and the US authorities.

Carlos Mesa Gisbert, a popular television journalist who was Goni's vice-president, took over the presidency and put the gas crisis to a referendum in July 2004. Voting was mandatory: refusing to cast a ballot would result in a prison sentence. There were four possible plans on the ballot and each voter was to choose one. The possibilities were to repeal the gas exportation plan, increase revenues with a new plan, use the gas plan to gain access to the Pacific through Chile, or use profits for social development. Very few voters understood the wording on the ballot. There was no clear question of whether to nationalize the gas companies.

Felipe Quispe from the Bolivian Farm Workers Federation and Jamie Solares of the Bolivian Workers' Union wanted full nationalization of hydrocarbon resources, and led blockades and protests against the referendum. Evo Morales, opposition leader, lobbied for nationalization. On July 18 it was announced that 75 percent of the voters favoured the referendum, but it never happened. Nothing was done about the gas crisis during Mesa's term.

By March 2005 the people lost patience once more and roadblocks and protests became the norm. Besides the gas crises, the people were angry because Gabriel Pinto, leader of the Bolivian Landless Movement (MST), was in jail for the June 14, 2004, lynching of the ruthless Ayo Ayo mayor Benjamin Altamirano. Four oil fields near Cochabamba were closed.

Mesa stated that Bolivia was ungovernable and offered to turn the presidency over to senate president Hormando Vaca Diez, an unpopular right-wing supporter of foreign investment. Evo Morales was the cause of the chaos, Mesa concluded.

Morales, Quispe and Solares demanded 50 percent royalties from the gas income and encouraged the strikes and protests. The government introduced a gas tax of 32 percent that was easily avoided by the multinationals. There were more marches and roadblocks, although Mesa was smart enough to keep the military from killing any more campesinos.

The subsequent round of negotiations and concessions compensated indigenous groups for any use of their land. This made foreign companies unhappy. They had been pumping money into Bolivian gas since 1996 and felt that the new agreement would jeopardize their investments. Lawsuits were threatened and the US suggested the IMF and World Bank would probably want to investigate.

The teachers' union called a strike, the peasants put up blockades, and the miners' union joined the teachers. Morales's MAS party organized a peasant march from Cochabamba to La Paz. By the end of May 2005 tens of thousands of protesters were in La Paz. Roads and airports were closed. Under duress, congress introduced a hydrocarbon law and increased royalties.

However, nothing short of nationalizing the gas companies would appease the peasants. On June 6 the country was again shut down. Mesa resigned and Eduardo Rodriguez Veltze, chief justice of the Supreme Court—and fourth in line for the presidency—became the interim president after the other three declined. He held office until an early election could be called. In December 2005, a victorious Evo Morales—the first fully indigenous president of Bolivia—stood on the palace balcony and waved to his hopeful people. The Movement Toward Socialism, MAS, had won an unprecedented 1,544,374 ballots, or 53.7 percent of the total electoral vote. Under the leadership of Evo Morales, the country moved with great hope for satisfactory solutions to social problems and economic growth.

Evo Morales

Evo was blessed during a religious ceremony at Tihuanaco, followed by his inauguration in La Paz the next day. The flamboyant performance brought "Evo Mania" to Bolivia—along with journalists, tourists, filmmakers and political analysts eager to see what was going to happen. He took office on January 22, 2006.

By May 2006 Evo had fulfilled his campaign promise and nationalized the oil industry. He bought back controlling stocks at world prices and then collected a higher tax from foreign investment, which increased revenues from US$320 million to US$780 million within the first year.

Recent studies indicate that Bolivia has 600 percent more gas than what was previously thought, with 85 percent near Tarija, 10 percent near Santa Cruz and the rest near Cochabamba. This amounts to about 1.5 trillion cubic metres, valued at US$120 billion. But even with newly negotiated prices, Bolivia continues to feel slighted. The country receives between US$3.15 and $3.50 per thousand cubic metres while the US receives between $5.85 and $7.90 per thousand.

Evo also introduced a land reform decree aimed at returning nonproducing land to landless campesinos. The Mennonites living in the Santa Cruz area are a bit uneasy about this, because the government doesn't seem to distinguish between unused land and land that the Mennonites are letting lie fallow for a year.

Evo's promise to amend the constitution with a two-thirds vote on each changed item has been slower in coming. The opposition has rejected many suggestions and Evo, as a compromise, has offered a majority vote to pass amendments. This too has been refused by Evo's opponents.

The many years of protests and demonstrations, culminating in Evo's victory, have given a sense of power to the people. A leader who represents the majority of the population of Bolivia—the indigenous Indians—is finally in charge. But cracks in their unity are getting wider. In 2007, the middle class Youth for Democracy group clashed with MAS supporters in Cochabamba, leaving 100 to 200 people injured and three dead. One group accused the other of infiltrating their meetings. The accusations escalated into a confrontation with both sides using baseball bats, pipe wrenches, sticks and dynamite against their political opponents.

Another crack is between Evo's *cocaleros* and the ordinary campesinos.
Everyone wants the US to take its drug war home. Most campesinos don't like the social decay caused by the use of illegal drugs, and for the most part stay away from both drugs and the drug trade; they feel it's a black mark on their culture when their compatriots produce drugs. But they don't see why the war should happen in Bolivia, where few actually use cocaine. The US, of course, wants the war to continue.

A third crack separates miners from one another. In October 2006, miners working for private companies and miners working for the government fought against each other, armed with exploding dynamite sticks. Sixteen were killed. The conflict arose from government workers making far less than those working in private enterprise.

Evo tried to strengthen indigenous culture by requiring all government employees to learn a native language by 2007. He also proposed that state schools teach indigenous languages; failure to do so would lose them their accreditation. For a country like Bolivia, this idea was far-fetched, but—fortunately—Evo has been willing to compromise. By mid-2006, he listened to opposition from non-indigenous groups and scrapped the indigenous-language instruction idea.

A rift between the western Altiplano areas, where socialism is popular, and the eastern lowlands, where western commerce is favoured, has also caused protests. Presently, there's a popular separation movement in the oil-rich Santa Cruz region. And even though Bolivia is getting more for its gas money, 70 percent of the people now want refining to occur in their country rather than in Chile or Argentina.

Conclusion

The IMF and World Bank economic plans did not work. In 2005, the poverty rate was 64 percent and climbing. Although unemployment was 7.6 percent in 2006, down from 14 percent in 2005, 35 percent of the population is still under-employed. Two-thirds of the national budget was eaten up by debt. Bolivia qualifies and receives support from the World Bank's Heavily

Indebted Poor Countries program. The US has sent over $150 million in aid, and Spain has written off $120 million of Bolivia's debt.

Waldo Albarracin, a human rights lawyer and president of Bolivia's Human Rights Commission, said that the problem is not bad intentions, but bad theory combined with institutional arrogance and lack of accountability to the people. According to Jim Schultz, the Democracy Center's executive director, the IMF and World Bank would likely defend their theories and lay blame on the implementation. We can just watch and listen to see what else will happen.

Despite all of Bolivia's tribulations, the country still draws travellers back time and time again. It is politically unstable, but it can be incredibly interesting if you're lucky enough to discuss politics and social movements with locals who are really in the know. If you can speak and understand some Spanish, you'll have a good chance of this.

15

PROTESTANT MISSIONARIES

Of Bolivia's total population, an overwhelming 78 percent are Catholic, 16 percent are Protestant, 3 percent are of non-Christian faiths and 2.5 percent have no religion. Chapter Four, "Colonial Religion," outlined the history of Catholicism and Jesuit missions in Bolivia. This chapter explores the non-Catholic religions and the missionaries who brought them to Bolivia.

Until 1967, Article Three of the Bolivian constitution kept Catholicism as the official religion of the country—in other words, until 1967 it was illegal to be anything but Catholic. Indigenous groups had learned to incorporate their own religious practices into the Catholic services. Until 2006, only the Catholic Church could legally provide public schooling. But religious classes—once compulsory—are now optional, and non-Catholic groups can teach in their own schools and offer medical services. A recent rise in indigenous cultural pride in Bolivia—and throughout the world—means that Aymara and Quechua religious ceremonies are now practised openly rather than surreptitiously.

Despite these advances, all non-Catholic groups must register with the Ministry of Foreign Affairs and Worship for permission to conduct religious services. This licence is very expensive and can take years of swimming in a legal cesspool before it is granted.

The first non-Catholic missionaries began arriving in Bolivia around 1883. They came from every Christian-based evangelizing country in the world. They brought bibles and good intentions, but were slow to be accepted. One of the failings of the Protestant movement was, and still is, its rigid Anglo-Saxonism. The austere Anglo-Saxon mannerisms and customs seemed so odd, unnatural and foreign to native Bolivians who had integrated their own ceremonies with the pomp of Catholicism that one priest declared it would be just as easy to convert the people to Mohammedanism as it was to Protestantism. To successfully convert, the Protestant churches would have to work on service rather than sermons.

Allen Gardiner, a British missionary from the Church of England, arrived in 1883. He embarked on an arduous trip (often on the back of a donkey) through Argentina up to Tarija, where he applied to the Bolivian government to "instruct them [Indians] in the Protestant religion in the hope of recovering them from their present abject condition." The reply was, "though the government was tolerably enlightened, the ignorance, intolerance and vices of the [Protestant] clergy were incredible and their influence sufficient to frustrate any attempt of so-called heretics to enlighten the Indians." Dissuaded, Gardiner went to Sucre where he convinced the government that he wasn't a heretic, and would work to help Indians in the colonies give up their nomadic and "heathen" lifestyles. However, before Gardiner could set up shop, the government was overthrown and the subsequent government upheld the Catholic-only rules. Gardiner moved on to Tierra del Fuego where he died of cold and starvation while trying to open more missions for Indians.

Canadian Baptist Archibald Reekie, inspired by God and a thirst for adventure, arrived in Oruro with his family knowing that evangelistic work was illegal. To get around the law he opened the first Protestant school in 1899 and used the bible as a teaching tool for English language instruction. He became the first Protestant educator in Bolivia and even managed to win the favour of a few Catholic authorities by attending Catholic Church meetings. Robert Routledge, a colleague and friend of Reekie's, opened a similar school in La Paz that same year, and then Reekie opened another one in Cochabamba.

The Reekies lived in Cochabamba under harsh discrimination from Catholics, occasionally facing drunken mobs throwing stones. Reekie is quoted as likening the Indians to "sheep without a shepherd." Besides confrontations by mobs, the Canadians found the altitude sickening, the road conditions isolating and the poverty inhibiting. They moved six times in six years in an attempt to alleviate some of their discomforts, all to no avail.

Irishman William Payne and his wife arrived in Cochabamba in 1902 after they had successfully established an evangelical church in Argentina. At the time the Bolivian government was in a heated debate on whether to permit freedom of religion or allow the continuation of the Catholic monopoly. Payne felt extreme pressure from Catholic priests and congregations who accused him of spreading a false religion. In September 1902 a mob lead by the priests burned his house and everything inside. Payne escaped, but even as he fled the city he promised a shipment of bibles. In response, the mob hurled stones and garbage at him. Payne sympathizers publicized the incident until parliamentary debate of the issue increased, resulting in constitutional reform and the passing of the Freedom of Worship Act in 1906. Civil marriages (non-church marriages) were then also permitted.

Methodists arrived soon after, opening several schools and some hospitals. Although the Freedom of Worship Act allowed religious freedom, restrictions on the Protestant organizations remained stringent.

By 1917 the Bible Society had arrived and reported that there were three Protestant missionary boards—Methodist Episcopal, Canadian Baptist and Bolivian Indian Mission—working in the country. At the time, the American Institute, modeled after American boys' boarding schools, was permitted to run private schools in Cochabamba and La Paz. Economic problems after World War II resulted in Canadian and American government cutbacks to these schools, and most closed.

Norman Dabbs, another Canadian Baptist, came to work in Oruro in 1949. He and his wife Lorna were evangelizing in the village of Melcamaya when a local mob, angry that the Baptists weren't taking part in time-honoured community feasts, stormed the mission hall and pelted those inside with stones and sticks. As they tried to escape, eight people were killed—including Norman—and six were seriously wounded, earning a spot in local history as the "Melcamaya Martyrs." Lorna, pregnant at the

time, escaped and returned to Canada where she continued to work with

the Baptist church. She died of natural causes in Prince George, British

Columbia, in 2007 at the age of 89. For a monument to the Dabbs, one has

to travel to Goderich, Ontario, to see the Norman Dabbs Lodge.

When the first twelve Mennonite families arrived in 1954 from Paraguay, they chose to live a peaceful and segregated life in the rain forests near
Santa Cruz—they did not come to convert. A second wave of 48 families
arrived in 1956. They cleared forests, planted soy, corn, sorghum and wheat
and eventually produced 75 percent of Bolivia's total soy crop. There was another immigration influx from Paraguay, Germany and Canada during the
1960s and 1970s. Today, the Mennonite population in the Santa Cruz area
has reached about 40,000 people living in 27 communities. At first, as dairy
farmers, the Mennonites produced tons of cheese but market prices made
production unprofitable beginning in the mid-1980s so they have reverted
to traditional crops. Mennonites still provide health care, orphanages, disaster relief and educational workshops on new agricultural methods for
locals outside their own religious community, although they do not tend to
intermarry.

Mennonite children are taught German at their own schools, and the
language is also used for religious services, but Mennonites speak Spanish
when in the community doing business. Mennonites stand out in Bolivia:
the men wear bibbed overalls and the women wear bonnets and plain, ankle-
length dresses. They mind their own business, help those in need, and tend
to face conflict peacefully. If travelling by bus in the Missions area of Santa
Cruz, there is a good chance you'll see them around.

Lastly, over 150,000 practising Mormons live in Bolivia. Most worship
in Cochabamba at one of the largest Mormon temples in the world. Since
the "Catholic only" laws changed in 1967, Mormons have been arriving in
droves. The Mormon missionaries are as easy to spot as the Mennonites.
They are most often young, spotlessly groomed North American men with
dark suits, white shirts done up to the collar, and black ties. They, like the
Mennonites, are generally polite and non-aggressive.

16

MODERN LIFE AND CULTURE

Population

In July 2007 Bolivia had 9,119,152 people, which was 1.42 percent more than the previous year. This places its population growth rate 99th out of 226 countries. As mentioned earlier, 60 percent of the nine million people are indigenous, and Quechua (2.5 million), Aymara (2 million) and Guarani (125,000) are the largest groups. Thirty percent of the population is of European background. During the Cerro Rico era, Africans were brought in as slaves and made up 5 percent of the total population. Today there is a very tiny pocket of African-Bolivians living just out of Coroico in the Yungas.

Government

Bolivia is a multi-party democratic republic with the president as head of state and head of government. National Congress, located in La Paz, has an upper house (Senate) and a lower house (Chamber of Deputies). Congress controls the money and can on some issues override the President, and even impeach him. The judiciary is independent of the government.

There are 27 seats in the Senate, represented by three constituents from each of the nine departments. Two of these three seats represent the winning party and the third represents the party receiving the second largest number of votes. Senators serve five-year terms and must be 35 years of age or more to qualify.

The Chamber of Deputies consists of 130 seats with 70 elected from single-member electoral districts. The remaining 60 are elected by proportional representation. Deputies serve five-year terms and must be 25 years or older on the day of election.

Local meals like this cost about 50 cents and are partly responsible for driving McDonald's (three outlets) out of Bolivia.

The country of Bolivia is made up of districts, which are then divided into provinces in which cities and towns are located. The districts fall under national elections, while towns and cities have municipal elections.

It is legal for anyone to form a political party and run in presidential elections. Voting is compulsory for everyone who is married and over the age of 18 and for those unmarried who are over 21. Women have been permitted to vote since 1938 and the Indians were given the vote after the 1952 revolution. Of the 3,671,152 registered voters in Bolivia, 92.6 percent cast valid votes in the 2005 election. Four percent of the ballots were blank.

As we've seen, Bolivian democracy doesn't mean much if the army feels threatened. Constitutional changes are relatively easy for presidents to achieve. But overall, democracy is growing.

Political Parties

As mentioned before, Movement Toward Socialism, or MAS (the acronym means "more" in Spanish), is headed by founding member and current Bolivian President Evo Morales, an indigenous coca farmer opposed to America's approach to their war on drugs in Bolivia. The party, formed in 1997, has socialistic leanings and a basic platform of nationalizing Bolivia's gas, oil and mineral rights.

The Social and Democratic Power, or Podemos (the almost-acronym means "we can"), is a right-wing pro-business party. Previously known as Accion Democratica Nacionalista (ADN), the party name was changed to Podemos upon the death of party leader Hugo Banzer because party members no longer wanted to be associated with the oppressive former president. Despite the re-branding, the policies and ideology of Podemos have not changed significantly from the days of the ADN.

The National Unity Front, a centre-right party, is headed by the popular 2005 presidential candidate Samuel Jorge Doria Medina Auza, a cement baron.

The four other parties represented during the 2005 election received 3.4 percent of the total votes.

Military Service

In Bolivia, holding power in government means controlling the military. There are over 35,000 military personnel, most conscripted for a minimum of one year. Males over 18 are required to serve, but when numbers fall short, the military conscripts those as young as 14 and keeps them longer than the required time. It's estimated that 40 percent of the military is under 18 and half of those are under 16. There is also a mandatory one-year pre-military instruction for men in the last year of secondary education, and for women living near Bolivia's international borders. Since 2001 women have been permitted to train in military colleges for two of the five-year basic officer training courses. They are not permitted to serve as officers. About 100,000 men became eligible in 2005 to serve as new recruits in the military.

Exemption is permitted for sons of widows, men with parents over 70, married or widowed men who have dependent families, disabled men, and miners working underground. Upon completion of service men receive a booklet proving their stint is over. Those unable to produce the booklet are hauled off to barracks and stuck into uniform. There is no such thing as a conscientious objector, but draft evasion is widespread. Those wishing to postpone their service can purchase a booklet for US$200 to $400 on the black market, or from corrupt military personnel. This privilege is affordable only to the wealthy Hildago kids. Booklets are required before a passport is issued or entrance to university is permitted.

The military budget is about US$135 million and covers 10 military regions throughout the nine departments. Bolivia signed the Inter-American Treaty for Reciprocal Assistance in 1947, but there has been no need to ask for military assistance from abroad as there have been no actual wars since the Chaco War. In the past the US has been heavily involved in training Bolivian military men at bases in the US. By June 2007—two years into Evo's "Movement Toward Socialism" government—the US state department explained their primary goal in Bolivia was "strengthening Bolivia's democratic institutions." Foreign Military Financing (FMF) funding was allocated to "provide essential support to Bolivian Army military police battalions, counterdrug units and a counterterrorist unit. FMF will be used to educate, train and equip a Bolivian Military Police Command." The funding supplies the police with items such as vehicles, weapons, ammunition and computers.

In May 2006 Hugo Chavez, president of Venezuela, claimed the US was "warming the ears" of Bolivian military personnel in hopes of inciting another coup. General Wilfredo Vargas, the commander in chief of the Bolivian Armed Forces, disclaims this statement.

Social Services and Benefits in Bolivia Today

Children in Bolivia must attend school until age 17 or until they finish grade eight, and the government's goal is for everyone to complete at least eight years of primary school. Presently, about 50 percent of the population completed primary school and 26 percent finished high school. In 1999, 16,000 students took university entrance exams but only 400 passed. Often the poor can't afford to pay the US$15 per month tuition (which goes toward the US$100 per month teachers' salaries), so the children don't go to school and there are no truant officers to insist on education. An estimated 800,000 children between the ages of 7 and 14 are illegally employed, often as domestics. Many farm kids don't make it to school at all.

Social benefits such as unemployment insurance, healthcare, and welfare are unavailable for farm workers, domestics or market stall operators.

This encompasses more than half of the population.

On the bright side, all women in their reproductive years are entitled to free medical care, as are children under age five. There is also a monthly milk allowance for children during the first year of life, and the schools also offer a milk program. As in most struggling societies, these social programs often fall apart due to corruption. A few years ago, bags of powdered milk designated for the schools could be purchased in the markets.

Andean woman with baby born in the tiny village of Pelechuco where no medical services can be found.

Extensive medical care is unaffordable to most Bolivians. Cleft palates and clubfeet, for example, are often neglected.

About 25 percent of all employed workers belong to a union and earn at least minimum wage, last raised in March 2006 to 660 *bolivianos* (US$85) per month for a 48-hour workweek. About 64 percent of the 9.1 million people live in poverty; they are either unemployed or working as domestics, farmers, or market vendors and don't fall under the minimum wage law. Generally, women earn less than men for the same work. Paid maternity leave is permitted for six weeks before and six weeks after the birth of the child for those employed 15 or more days per month. The recipient gets the national minimum wage and 70 percent of her wages above that. Women are also protected from dismissal after the birth for a period of one year.

A universal pension plan was implemented in 2003, but with so many people born in a country where birth registration is not always possible, the government is in a quagmire of paperwork trying to get the money to eligible recipients who have reached 65. Employers must pay family allowances to employees for children between age 1 and 19. (Of course, the larger the family, the more difficult it is to get a job.)

Crime and Human Rights

According to the official report Bolivia sent to Interpol in 2000, crime in Bolivia is comparatively low. In 2000 (according to the most recent statistics) there were 2,558 murders; 1,809 sex offences; 4,931 serious assaults; 8,762 thefts and 8,377 aggravated thefts. Of these crimes, 14 percent were committed by females and 5.1 percent by juveniles. (Interestingly, 18 percent of fraud charges were attributed to females.) For a slightly more recent comparison, the 2002 US homicide rate was 5.6 homicides for every 100,000 people; in Bolivia, the homicide rate was 2.82.

Violent crimes involving visitors are low, although petty theft such as pickpocketing is common. With all my travelling, I have found that Bolivia is one of the safest countries in the western hemisphere; a vendor once chased after me to return some change she'd forgotten to give me. However, caution should be taken no matter where one travels (including traditionally safe places like Canada!).

Human rights violations are still a concern. Most abuses occur during clashes between the military or police and the often-protesting peasants. In these cases, any abuse charges brought against the military are tried in military court, and therefore are usually dismissed without conviction.

While arbitrary arrest or detention without charges being laid is no longer common, incarceration on trumped-up charges is widespread. Whether the charge is warranted or not, internment can last months or even years before the suspect is brought to trial. Bribery helps spin the legal wheel faster. About 30 percent of Bolivian prisoners spend more time in custody waiting for their court day than they do serving out their sentences. The government does not force investigations into alleged abuses in the jails, so once the police become involved in a case, the accused have little recourse unless they have the money to pay bribes.

Prisons are harsh, overcrowded and often life-threatening for those without access to money. San Pedro Prison in La Paz, where curious tourists can play at being incarcerated for a few days, has between 8,000 and 12,000 prisoners in a space designed for less than 5,000. Inmates (and visiting tourists) must purchase or rent cells that cost between US$20 (per month) and $5,000 (if purchased). If they cannot afford this, they sleep in the prison hallways or exposed courtyard. The small, less expensive cells are about 1 metre by 1.5 metres by 2 metres (3 x 5 x 6 feet), with no ventilation, lighting or furniture. Some prisoners must sleep sitting up, and serious anemia due to lack of nutritional food is common. Free medical care is unavailable but as with everything else in prison, if the prisoner has money he can purchase what he needs. "Troublesome" prisoners may experience cell fires—later reported as "an accident." Those with money have access to good food (there are upscale restaurants inside San Pedro prison), warm clothing, illegal drugs and expensive booze. It is a society within a society. Some lucky prisoners can get jobs within the prison as waiters, dishwashers, housekeepers and medical providers, and some are drug dealers. Sex at bargain prices is always available.

Children under the age of six are permitted to live in the prison with an incarcerated parent. At present there are 665 children in San Pedro. Because many of them would end up living on the street, they are routinely allowed to stay after age six as their parents serve their sentences.

Low wages and the class system contribute to widespread corruption in the judicial system. In 2006 Bolivia rated 105th on a list of 163 countries on the Transparency International Corruption Perceptions Index, rating 2.7 out of 10. Any value under 3.0 translates to rampant corruption throughout the country. (For comparison, Haiti rated 1.8 and Canada received an 8.5. Finland came out as the least corrupt country, with a rating of 9.6.)

Although every Bolivian is granted the right to assembly—and Bolivians exercise this right often—the press is not permitted to criticize the government or the church, and quoting an unnamed source is not allowed. References to homosexuality and obscenities are also frowned upon. Violators are subject to two months in prison, which, as we've seen, could extend indefinitely if bribe money is lacking.

Gender roles are specific and same-sex relationships are widely ridiculed. Although having a private life is a constitutional right, intense discrimination against gays from the morally upright Catholic society is prevalent. Gay rights demonstrations always result in harassment and any suspected homosexuals caught by the police are made to pay "fines" for fake charges, with the money landing directly into the pockets of low-paid police—any resistance results in exposure and shame to the families. The topic of homosexuality is not discussed. Most gays marry and have children and then conduct clandestine encounters when they can. The government attempted to pass a same-sex marriage law in 2004, but strong opposition resulted in the law being abandoned. Recent reports, however, show that discrimination against indigenous soldiers in the military has decreased substantially.

Prostitution is legal for those 18 and older, but child prostitution is rampant nonetheless. At present, about 2,000 prostitutes working mainly in La Paz and Santa Cruz are registered with the authorities. (The advantage of registering is that the girls are given free socially transmitted disease testing every three months.) Of course, many prostitutes are not registered, especially not the child prostitutes. In 2005, there were about 7,000 cases of AIDS in patients between the ages of 15 and 49. In 2006, there were just under 500 AIDS-related deaths. Due to limited resources, the medical profession is only able to treat the symptoms. Human trafficking is increasing, especially in areas like El Alto, where children are abducted and exported to surrounding countries and then forced into domestic labour and prostitution. Last year 44 human trafficking cases were investigated but there were no convictions.

While condoms and birth control pills are available at pharmacies and do not require prescriptions, over 100 abortions are performed every day at the Women's Hospital in La Paz. Bolivia's "abortion" law specifies that a miscarriage must already be in progress before the woman enters the clinic. (Abortion is only legal with judicial authorization, and only if the woman's life or health is at risk.) Once at the hospital, she has to claim that the miscarriage is natural, and doctors are then allowed to fix what she started. Because of this law, dangerous home remedies and visits to illegal abortionists are common. Many women die from complications such as infection or excessive bleeding. A woman convicted of having an unauthorized abortion gets three years in prison. Her doctor gets six.

Discrimination against women, indigenous people and Afro-Bolivians is present in Bolivia. Sixty-two percent of women experience domestic violence at least once in their lives, as compared to seven percent in Canada. Four out of five illiterate people in Bolivia are women. Bolivian criminal law states that the act of rape is not a crime—it only becomes a crime once it is reported. Having an indigenous president is challenging discrimination in Bolivia, although Evo has more than once been called an "uppity Indian" by non-Indians.

Lustrabotas ("Shoeshine Boys")

The ubiquitous shoeshine boys, found on every downtown street in most Bolivian cities, wear wool balaclavas to hide their identities and to protect themselves from air pollution. They are as young as seven years old, yet working to help support themselves and their families. Those without families often sleep in cleaned-out tombs in cemeteries or under a piece of cardboard behind garbage dumps. Police harassment is rampant; usually they accuse the boys of drug abuse (although only about 10 percent are guilty of this).

Magazine and newspaper articles written about these children have resulted in aid and intervention by numerous national and international social groups such as Qharuru, Global Impact and UNICEF. Their programs require the children to study a few hours every day in exchange for safe sleeping places, nutritional food, and lockers in which the kids store their shoeshine supplies while they sleep, eat or hit the books. These organizations also provide drug prevention programs.

For the traveller, whether you let the *lustrabotas* shine your boots and sandals is up to you. As with most people working on the streets in Bolivia, the *lustrabotas* are not aggressive. These boys are trying to make a living. I know of no scams or dangers when dealing with them and when I have stopped to speak to them, they have been courteous and cooperative.

Lustrabotas cover their faces while working to protect their health and identity.

Miners Today

The mining industry still plays a large part in Bolivian life and culture. A visit to Cerro Rico in Potosi is one of the best ways to see a working mine and gain a sense of what mining means to Bolivians today.

Locals say that mining left over 5,000 tunnels in Cerro Rico, forming such a labyrinth that visitors must use a knowledgeable guide to take them through without becoming lost. Tourists are encouraged to purchase coca leaves, fuel, boots, dynamite, clothing or anything else the miners are selling to help supplement their income. (I avoided the dynamite.)

Now run mostly as independent cooperatives, the mines, even with all their improvements, don't look like attractive places to work. The tunnels are still claustrophobically narrow, the stairs ill repaired, the air stifling hot. Some mines such as Rosario Bajo and Candalaria are built on five levels and run down 200 metres (600 feet), while others go 480 metres (1,500 feet) and pass as many as 17 levels on the way. The major difference from the early days is that now miners are looking for silver, lead, zinc and tin instead of just silver or tin.

Seventy percent of the mining at Cerro Rico is still done by traditional manual methods. To become an independent miner, a man must obtain a jackhammer and drill, which togeth-er cost anywhere from US$1,000 to $4,000. More sophisticated labour-saving machinery costs up to US$20,000—out of reach for most Bolivians—so many men form co-operatives and pool their resources to purchase gear. In 2007 there were 10,000 miners and a total of 60,000 workers, employed in 350 cooperatives and 18 private compa-nies located in Potosi, Oruro and La Paz. Five hundred men presently work supplying 46 private, interna-tionally owned processing plants. In

Chollas arriving at Isla del Sol, Lake Titicaca. Derbies or bowler hats have been traditional dress since the 1920s.

Miners exchange coca often donated to them by tourists.

February 2007, Evo Morales moved another socialist step closer to nationalization by confiscating the only operating smelter in the country, a Swiss-owned business near Oruro whose largest stockholder is ousted president Sanchez de Lozada—Goni.

Even though the minimum age for working is 14, miners can apprentice at age 12. They start with three years of lugging 20-kilo packs of ore to the pulley shafts that haul the rock to the surface. Depending on how much they carry and the quality of the ore, apprentices earn between US$4 and $8 for a 12-hour day. After three years these teenage boys can prospect independently.

When a miner finds a vein, the word spreads through the tunnels faster than light. The finder becomes rich overnight, enabling him to purchase a house and car and still have enough cash to never work again. The lure of glitter sustains them.

Coca also keeps them going. Miners' cheeks protrude with coca leaves, which numbs the stomach, suppresses the appetite and helps them bear discomfort (lunch buckets are often not included in a miner's equipment). Silicosis, stomach ailments, arthritis and tuberculosis are the most common health disorders, and the danger of dying from poisonous gases released from a lead or zinc vein is also very real. Odours can be detected easily, but escape must happen within 15 seconds or the nervous system paralyzes. At Cerro Rico, getting out of the narrow tunnels and up a rickety set of stairs to the outside would take a man on the lower levels at least 45 minutes. Gas masks are not available.

Visitors will notice bloodstains at the mine entrance. Twice a year, up to 40 llamas are sacrificed to protect the men working underground. There is also a shrine with a statue of the Virgin Mary where miners offer their possessions in return for safety. Inside, a sacred deity called Tio, made of straw and cloth and covered in ribbons, also looks after the men. Tio (which means "uncle")

Potosi Miner's Profile

Weekly salary — US$40 to $135

Education — 20% have completed less than 8 years of primary school; 56% have completed 8–12 years of school; 23% have some post-grade school education.

Average age — 23.5 years

Married — 50%

Push railway cars by hand (loaded cars weigh 1–2 tons each) — 30%

Make dynamite holes ready for blasting — 66%

Work on the pulley system — 16%

Manual labourers — 40%

Miners receive 10% of all tour money earned in Potosi.

receives gifts of candles, coca leaves, llama pieces, alcohol, cigarettes and paper streamers. And every Friday, miners stop to ask Tio for guidance.

The second deity living underground is Diable—the devil, recognized by his goat's beard, horns and red skin. Diable is bad luck, so he, too, is appeased with gifts. Women are considered the worst kind of bad luck and are prohibited from working underground, although female tourists may visit.

Laguna Verde turns a bright green when midday winds stir up arsenic in the water.

The Altiplano shows its natural rainbow of colour.

Parinacota and Pomerata, the Twin Sister Volcanoes are located just across the border in Chile.

Twin Sister Volcanoes overshadow this stone chapel.

Opposite: A woman from Potola, a village above Tarabuco, comes to market once a week.

Above: Woven with llama wool, Andean weavings contain images of local life.

Right: This ready-made Carnival costume costs about US$150 but some cost as much as $500.

Opposite: Revellers head home mid-morning after a night of festivities.

Above: Despite the size of a toucan's bill, it weighs very little.

Left: Locally made pottery with ancient and modern designs.

Opposite: Fresh spices available at La Paz Market.

Overleaf: Tile art shows an indigenous family.

17

CUSTOMS AND TRADITIONS

Weavings

A trip to Bolivia is not complete without learning about traditional weaving. The textile museum in La Paz has a moderate collection of Bolivian weavings, some very old, but the Indigenous Art Museum in Sucre has a full collection in addition to weavers demonstrating the two most common styles in Bolivia. You can also purchase weavings from street vendors throughout the highlands, from weavers' co-ops or directly from the museum in Sucre.

Andean weavings are made from either llama, alpaca or sheep (and rarely vicuña) wool. The wool is hand-dyed and woven into designs that date back to times before Christ. It is common to see women spinning wool and then combining two thin strands to form a thicker one. These strands are then dyed with chemicals or coloured with plant extractions, although natural dyes are rarely used today. After the wool is coloured, the women spin it to produce a crepe twist, a yarn that is both strong and elastic.

Most textiles are woven on the heddle loom, set outside. The other loom commonly used is the back-strap loom. Bolivian textiles have four selvages because weavers use a continuous warp. Designs, like those seen on Tihuanacan pottery, are of zoomorphic or anthropomorphic iconography and indicate the social status of the weaver. The colours and positions of the stripes are usually artistic preference. In the highlands, men weave belts on a lap-loom for their wives or girlfriends.

Many traditional weavings done by Potola Indian women on ancient looms can't be duplicated, even when using a computer to figure out the patterns. The colours are strong, the threads tight, the patterns unique and the prices far below international market value.

Weaving has been an art in the Andes for about 3,000 years.

Women's Fashion

Due to the cold high altitude, hats have always been worn in the Andes. During the mid-1800s, a shipment of bowler hats arrived by mistake from the Borsalini factory in Italy. An ingenious salesman bought them all and tried to sell them to the men, to no avail. He then told the Indian women that the hats were fertility hats. They became so popular that a factory in Sucre opened in 1929, which caused the price of hats to drop so that every woman could afford one. Now you won't find many Indian ladies without one perched to the side or back of her head in a cheeky manner.

Somehow the Indian ladies also locked into 19th century-style European shawls. These are great embroidered and tasseled garments worn over their shoulders and kept in place with an ornamental stickpin made of Potosi silver. Their skirts have numerous layers of material, each made from four or six yards of material gathered at the waist, accentuating the hips. The skirts fall well below the knees and conceal petticoats worn underneath, made with almost as much cloth as the skirts. On their feet, despite the rugged terrain of the cobbled roads or fields, most indigenous women wear pumps. I wore hiking boots under my full-skirted dress, and the women would respond with surprise and laugher. One lady felt so sorry for me that she offered to give me a pair of pumps. She also wanted to trade my skirt for hers. (Although North American dress is totally acceptable in Bolivia, I was wearing a full circle, tiered and gathered red dress that hangs from the shoulders to the ankle.)

Ruthuchiku – Hair Cutting Ceremony

Children often go unnamed until a suitable person—a *patrón*—can be chosen to provide a good solid name. The *patrón* becomes the second mother or father for the child, similar to a godparent but with far more responsibility (such as paying the child's tuition!). On the child's first birthday, a fiesta that can last up to 20 days is held. The house is cleaned and a piece of woven llama wool material, called an *ikuña*, is placed beside a pair of scissors. The second mother will call the spirits of the house to keep the child safe. She then cuts a lock of hair from the child's head, wraps it into a 100-*boliviano* bill and puts it into the llama wool weaving. She will then have a drink and pass the cutting ritual on to the next person at the party until all the child's hair is sitting on the weaving, with each piece wrapped in money. The *patrón* then announces the child's name.

Quinceañera

In Latin America, the *Quinceañera* ("fifteen years") is a girl's coming of age ceremony, comparable to a sweet sixteen party or a debutante ball marking a young woman's entrance into society. From my observations, a Bolivian *Quinceañera* celebration is almost as elaborate as a wedding. The girl's parents and her *patrón* save their money for years so they can spare no expense for the big event. On her 15th birthday, the young girl wears an exquisite evening gown and tiara and parades around to different picture-postcard sites in the community so everyone can see her and professional photographs can be taken. The birthday girl is accompanied by a court of seven boys and seven girls, attired in equally impressive outfits. In La Paz, the girls often walk the Bridge of the Americas and then dine with family and friends at an expensive restaurant. Following dinner, a special cake—topped with a doll wearing an identical *Quinceañera* dress—is served.

El Robo

El Robo (the robbery) is a ceremonial elopement originally associated with the urban and rural poor but now considered fashionable with the upper and middle-class Bolivians. If you get invited to one, be sure to go! The *robo* dates back to the days of the big estates, when an elopement was pre-arranged with the girl's and boy's families and, originally (and most importantly), with the *patrón* of the estate. The *robo*, which is almost a ritual skit, is staged at a party. After the boy and girl spend some days (and nights) together, the groom formally "apologizes" to the girl's family, and is led by her family to the government office where the licence is acquired. After this, the marriage proceeds as usual. *Robos* are mostly great parties, involving cake-judging competitions, dancing, marathon drinking, and lots of roastings, mainly of the groom. At their best, they allow for amicable separations if either party has second thoughts. At their worst, especially if they're not carefully arranged, they can lead to arguments that escalate to violence and even murder. A father, brother, or uncle is traditionally held "responsible" for seeing that the sister, daughter or niece is treated with respect as they consider the marriage. Because *patróns* of the estate are less common these days, there is no one to mediate a peaceful resolution for both parties, and long-term family feuds can result.

Dry-Run Marriage

Since 1952, Bolivian weddings often involve a civil ceremony first, with the church ceremony occurring up to a year later. There are two reasons for this: first, it is considered unlucky to be married during an odd-numbered year, so impatient and in-love couples have a civil marriage but postpone the church wedding for a year, and second, the civil ceremony is taken more as a dry run, giving bride and groom a chance to reconsider before facing God.

Bachelor Friday

Viernes de Soltero (Bachelor Friday) is really for married men. On this weekly occasion, men are entitled to behave like bachelors by getting drunk and, if so inclined, conducting affairs or buying sex—either at the bar itself, which keeps girls for rental, or at a brothel. Behind this popular institution is the rationale that Latin Americans have a more reasonable approach to monogamy and fidelity. Bachelor Friday is mainly for men who regard affairs as normal, but for married women, I suppose the affairs could end in disaster.

Motels

The word comes from North America, but the place is only indirectly related to automobile travel. This is where the better-off Bolivians (those who have cars) come to conduct affairs. Usually motels are enclosed compounds with ticket wickets. You pay by the hour, drive in, and the gate closes so that your car is out of sight. Motel signs indicate their purpose; the word "motel" is accompanied by images of Cupid, linked hearts or nude couples embracing.

Teas

Teas are essentially a coffee klatch or tea party for women, often accompanied by card games (canasta is big) and always accompanied by gossip. For whites and upper-class mestizos, teas are sometimes held at certain cafés, such as Casa del Corregidor in Le Paz. *Chollas* (indigenous women in traditional dress) have teas too, usually while working, and their tribal and family connections extend to women of their class in general. *Cholla* teas can become what is more like a labour union, expressing itself in political actions like boycotts, protests, and party or candidate rallies. *Chollas* have pulled off some of the biggest pro-union demonstrations and anti-hunger marches in Bolivian history—many of them organized at these teas.

Q'owa

This coca leaf ceremony, practised on the first Friday of every month, is probably the most traditional and popular ceremony within the indigenous population. Small sugar charms representing love, health, travel or financial success are purchased and burned along with coca, quinoa, seeds, eggs and llama wool. Before the burning starts, participants chew coca and give thanks to Pachamama, Inti and Killa (Mother Earth, Sun and Moon), from whom everything comes. Once the burning is well under way, alcohol is dripped onto the four corners of the fire vessel (usually a tiny barbeque-style burner). The four corners represent the cardinal points and the burning signifies the giving and taking of life. Pachamama is fed, and in turn she will provide for those who believe in her.

Alasista (January 24th)

Alasista, which means "buy from me" in Aymara, is a celebration also known as the Festival of Abundance. Worshippers climb the stairs of the Stations of the Cross (each station represents one of the humiliations Christ suffered before his crucifixion) and pray to Ekeko, a stout, smiling dwarf who is the god of fertility, happiness and prosperity. Ekeko is depicted as a miniature doll loaded with tiny dollar bills, musical instruments, food, coca leaves, vehicles—anything a person may want. According to tradition, an Ekeko doll laden with specific objects of desire should be purchased at noon on the 24th. He is then blessed in a ceremony that uses alcohol, confetti, paper streamers and candy, followed by a dousing of Holy Water. The hope is that the items your Ekeko carries are what you will be blessed with during the year.

Interestingly, *Alasista* was originally an Aymara celebration of the spring equinox, in honour of the coming crops. The Spaniards changed the date of the celebration to the end of January, hoping to be rid of the pagan custom. In retaliation, the Aymara made the festival into a mockery by creating Ekeko and loading him up with every conceivable item that could be purchased, thus mocking the greed of the Spanish.

Alasista lasts for two weeks, during which time La Paz has the largest handicraft fair in the country. It is held in the old zoo, with 10,000 merchants from as far away as Argentina and Peru bringing everything from live llamas, horses and alpacas to traditional handicrafts. This is a great place to purchase weavings, jewellery, leather goods, wood carvings, books, paintings, sculptures and crystal, and it's also an opportunity to taste some of the more special dishes of La Paz such as *chairo*, a freeze-dried potato cooked in a lamb soup, or *plato Paceño*—corn, cheese, beans and potatoes cooked together as a stew.

Carnival

Forty days before Easter—usually near the end of February—is the week-long celebration known as *Carnival*. Wednesday, Thursday and Saturday of *Carnival* week are celebrated with dancers in elaborate and expensive costumes (some priced as high as US$500) and masks parading through the cities. Friday is solemn: everyone is forbidden to dance or drink alcohol. Saturday is officially water fight day, and no one is spared. (The water fights actually start about a month before *Carnival* and escalate in frequency.) The custom is to chuck *globos* (balloons) half-filled with water at anyone and everyone, tourists included. Market ladies fill and sell buckets of balloons all day long. Before balloons were available, the revellers threw confetti-filled eggshells. Dumping buckets of water from windows and balconies onto people below is also customary; I watched one group of young girls do this non-stop for the entire day. During the 2003 *Carnival*, 11 deaths were attributed to the over-exuberance of the festivities, and some officials are trying to abolish the use of *globos*, but I doubt that will happen. Just remember

that during *Carnival*, rain gear is essential.

On *Carnival* Monday, flowers are planted as a symbol of spring. Tuesday, the last day of the celebrations, is called *Ch'alla*, when everything in a Bolivian home, including personal possessions, is blessed and sprinkled with wine specially made for the event. The people also decorate their houses with streamers and throw confetti on each other. Everyone visits and shares *chicha*.

Las Chutas is a Bolivian tradition of making fun of the Spanish

Oruro has the largest *Carnival* celebrations in Bolivia.

with dance, costumes and skits during the entire *Carnival* week. Oruro has the most extensive *Carnival*, known for its world-famous parade. Hotel rooms and reservations for seats at the stadium where the parade culminates must be booked months in advance.

Dia del Mar

March 23 marks the death of Eduardo Avaroa, a hero from the War of the Pacific. As mentioned in Chapter 6 in the "Hilarión Daza and War of the Pacific" section (page 93), Avaroa is remembered as saying, "Surrender? Only when you give up your grandmother!" before he was killed in the Battle of Topàter. March 23 also marks Bolivia's loss of its coastal land to Chile, so celebrations include a parade of government officials, peasants and children who, during the day, vow to reclaim the land that was lost during the war.

Semana Santa

This is the Easter holiday throughout Latin America. The date changes every year, but is always at the end of March or beginning of April. Although the celebration is held throughout Bolivia, the most interesting way to observe the tradition is to participate in the pilgrimage (called a *peregrinacion*) from La Paz to Copacabana, a distance of 158 kilometres (95 miles). *Peregrines* walk the entire distance starting on Good Friday and arriving mid-day Saturday. They then climb the Stations of the Cross on the hill overlooking Copacabana, confess all their sins and finally enter the cathedral in the centre of town where they are blessed for their sacrifice. Because Christ died on a Friday, the *peregrines* are permitted to steal food from the fields along the walk. When they finally arrive in Copacabana, they are a sorry sight. Most *peregrines* do the pilgrimage only once in a lifetime, but some do it once every three years. (Three is symbolic of the days between Christ's death and resurrection.)

Although car blessings occur in Copacabana every Sunday all year long, it is very special to have a vehicle blessed during *Semana Santa*. The lineup at the cathedral can stretch for miles. (See Chapter 4.)

There is no alcohol consumption on Saturday of *Semana Santa*, but the Sunday church service is followed by lots of feasting and sipping of *chicha*. The blessed vehicles are showered with their share of the spirits also.

Gran Poder

"The Great Power" is held in La Paz during a weekend in June (it changes yearly). This event is almost as extravagant as *Carnival* is in Oruro. First celebrated in 1939 as a candlelight procession in El Alto with a statue of Christ at the front, the event has grown to encompass everyone living in La Paz. Instead of a candlelight procession, *Gran Poder* is now a parade with elaborate costumes, traditional dancing and fiestas.

Festival of *Todos Santos*

All Saints' Day, or the "Day of the Dead," is in remembrance of deceased ancestors. It takes place each year on November 1 and 2. Laden with special cakes, breads and candies, locals visit the cemetery—often accompanied by a band—and offer their ancestors the goodies. It is believed that the spirits come back to earth at noon on November 1, and return to the beyond 24 hours later. The celebrators also place plastic wreaths, flowers and ribbons on the tombstones.

Festival Dances

During all Bolivian festivals where parades and dancing occur, you'll see dancers wearing bastardized imitations of clothes worn in court during the reign of Philip II in the 17th century. The dancers satirize Spanish lords doing the minuet.

The *Waca Tokhoris* ("dancing bulls") is performed by a dancer wearing a stuffed bull's head and a dried bull skin covered with traditional woven clothes. The "bull" is accompanied by a milkmaid who carries a tin jar typical of the old milk vendors, and together the two figures dance through the streets.

The Dance of the Devil is the most popular because of the elaborate costumes. The devil, or *diable* (sometimes called *"tio"* (uncle), is the guardian of Bolivian mines, and the featured dancer of most festivals; during *Carnival* he is the star.

Traditional Foods

Desayuno is the word for breakfast. My favourite is a fried egg placed inside a *panacita*. These can be purchased for a small fee in any restaurant patronized by locals.

Almuerzo is the main meal of the day, served from noon until two. Special restaurants make *almuerzo del dia* for a reasonable price; usually just a couple of dollars. It includes a spiced drink, a soup with noodles, some meat, some vegetables, some potatoes, and a dessert. Not all *almuerzo del dia* recipes are the same; sometimes black, red or blue potatoes are substituted for the white ones, or french fries are also popular. Sometimes the dessert is nothing more than a dish of Jell-O. There is almost always a sign outside the door of the restaurant advertising what is being served.

Cena is supper and is usually a light meal served well after seven in the evening.

Panacitas are fresh crusty rolls made with heavy rye flour. If purchased early in the morning, they are usually hot.

Maté de coca, a tea made with coca leaves, is mild and available in every restaurant. The tea is believed to stave off altitude sickness. This may be due to a chemical in the coca or because you are getting some of the four litres of water you should be drinking every day to acclimatize to the high altitude.

Chicha is a beer brewed from aysuma and waltaco, varieties of yellow corn. (There are about 220 varieties of corn grown in Bolivia.) *Chicha* is believed to be a drink of the gods. When made with a black corn, it is accompanied with a meal of strawberries and cinnamon ice cream.

Salteñas are a pastry stuffed with spiced meat and vegetables. They are the original fast food of Bolivia—get in line!

Laguas is a tasty corn soup.

Chejchi is a speckled grey and white corn that is toasted and eaten with butter. Available from street vendors.

Wiphala

The *Wiphala* is the Aymara Flag, a seven-coloured checkered cloth that has been the symbol of fraternity, reciprocity, and diversity for over 500 years. Squares of blue, green, red, yellow, orange and black run above and below a diagonal, white centre strip. The traditional Inca Flag, over 2,000 years old, is six stripes (rather than squares) and does not feature the white centre strip. You will see the Aymara Flag throughout Bolivia at festivals and in

The *Kantuta*, the national flower (same colours as the flag) comes from an Inca love story. Where the heroine died is where the first plant bloomed.

such places as Tihuanaco or El Fuerte, but you will not see the striped one unless you visit Peru.

Kantuta

The *Kantuta*, the national flower, displays the same colours as the Bolivian flag. The chalice-shaped flower has a red cup with a yellow sepal that attaches to the green plant. The legend of the *Kantuta* is an Inca love story well worth knowing: a vacationing king and his daughter Kento travelled to Copacabana, where they rested before proceeding to the Island of the Sun. In Copacabana Kento fell in love with a peasant, but knew that marriage would never be permitted. The night before Kento and her father were to leave for the island, the daughter snuck out to meet her lover for what she somehow knew would be the last time. The night was dark with no moon or stars to light the way. Tragically, she fell into a crevasse and died. On the spot where her body was found, a new and strange plant grew, and so the people called the plant *kentuta pankara*, which means "the flower of Kento's house."

18

TOURISM AND THE ENVIRONMENT

Some tourists might avoid Bolivia because of the political problems, but it is actually one of the safest and cheapest destinations in the world. Tourists in Bolivia—there were 335,000 in 2002—spend about US$200 million a year. (Compare this to the four million tourists who visit Cancun each year.) The upside of this is that Bolivia has few internationally operated tourism ventures, so most of the tourist dollars spent within the country go directly to the local people.

In this final chapter, we cover the standard material found in traditional tour guides: parks and recreation and the highlights of the Bolivian landscape. We start with the story of an iconic tourist, and end with some thoughts on environmentally responsible tourism.

Yossi Ghinsberg, Celebrity Tourist

Yossi Ghinsberg is one of Bolivia's most famous tourists, and has inspired many a traveller to follow in his adventurous footsteps. Ghinsberg, an Israeli, met Karl, an Austrian expat and guide, in La Paz in 1982. Karl promised to take Ghinsberg and two of his friends down the Tuichi river to a remote Indian village. On the way they'd pan for gold, of which there was rumoured to be much. Ghinsberg paid his shekels and packed his gear. They trekked through the jungle for days but got nowhere. The village never appeared, and neither did the gold. They were tired and hungry. So the four men commissioned some locals to build a balsa raft on which they would float down the Tuichi River to Rurrenabaque (often called Rurre), where they could catch a bus or plane back to La Paz.

The wild river proved to be far too difficult for the inexperienced adventurers, so Karl and one of Ghinsberg's friends decided to return on foot to their starting point. They were never seen again.

Bolivia has discovered that tourists like pizza.

Ghinsberg and his buddy Kevin, an American, continued on the raft. Within hours the riverbanks had closed in and risen hundreds of feet above the churning waters. The current became swifter as they found themselves approaching the non-navigable San Pedro Canyon, with its raging rapids and thundering waterfalls. The furious current kept them in the centre of the river until the raft struck a rock and they were thrown into the water. Kevin managed to get to shore in time to watch Ghinsberg clinging to a log as he dropped over the edge.

Ghinsberg held on as he was battered against rocks and almost drowned in the relentless waves. Finally, he was washed onto a small gravel beach where he counted his bruises and his blessings. Nothing was broken. After resting, Ghinsberg headed downriver looking for trails that would lead somewhere—anywhere—out of the god-forsaken hell he was in. He was eaten by termites, bitten by red Abuna ants and licked by a jaguar (but luckily he didn't smell or taste too good at that point). He sank into quicksand and was missed by what he had hoped was a search plane droning overhead. Kevin—who had made it to Rurre after staggering though the jungle for 20 days—took a day of rest and then hired guide

Tico Tudela to take him upriver looking for Ghinsberg. They found him alive.

Ghinsberg wrote a book, *Back from Tuichi*, soon after his ordeal, and now hundreds of admiring Israelis try to emulate his voyage (while hoping to avoid the life-threatening aspects). The book was translated into English, so thousands of English-speaking adventurers have turned up too. The sleepy fishing village of Rurre has since turned into a tourist mecca, with paved streets, coffee shops, Internet cafés, dozens of hotels and wild bars.

Tourist guides have made a few amendments to Yossi's trip. Extensive wildlife is viewed from the safety of a motorboat. The canyon is bypassed. In their downtime, tourists can read a photocopy of Ghinsberg's book purchased in Rurre (no enforceable copyright laws in Bolivia) for about US$25. For the less adventuresome, river trips farther down the Beni to the Yacuma River and the Nature Sanctuary are every bit as rewarding and far less dangerous. On both rivers, numerous pink, freshwater dolphins dive out of the muddy streams while capybaras, 120-pound guinea pigs, wallow in the mud along the shore, watching tourists float by. Caimans (a Central and South American crocodilian reptile) and exotic birds with colourful plumage are so abundant they go unnoticed after a few days. A walk through the nearby swamp with a guide may produce an anaconda or cobra for observation.

The big controversy now is whether wild creatures, particularly anacondas, should be handled by tourists. Tour companies want so much to please their clients—and get their business—that they take the chance of allowing tourists to handle snakes. I saw a man nervously grasp a snake so tightly it puked up a half-digested frog and mouse when it was finally released. The clutching was obviously traumatic, not to mention a waste of food. A no-touch style of eco-travel is recommended (although, with snakes, no touch is almost always no-see, as they must be dredged out of the swamp to be examined). Bolivians are increasingly becoming more concerned about the environment, and only time will tell whether or not the government is able to get a handle on habitat destruction. In the meantime, there are numerous NGOs and conservationist groups working hard to preserve what makes the country so beautiful.

Parks

Of Bolivia's total landmass, 19.4 percent is occupied by national parks, wilderness areas or nature reserves (there are a total of 32!) although only 15 parks are patrolled or managed by full-time wardens. This leaves vast wilderness areas open to poaching and logging. Nine parks have over a million hectares and most are in remote and difficult-to-reach regions.

The parks are diverse, found at elevations between sea level and 4,300 metres (14,000 feet), and with every terrain—from delicate mountain alpine to dry salt flats—and in climates that produce desert, rain forest, and humid jungle. With this varied environment the wildlife is tremendous. You can see over 17,000 species of plants, 316 species of mammals, 257 species of reptiles, 162 species of amphibians and 504 species of birds, both resident and migratory.

Numerous groups handle park protection; some are effective, others are not. The Proteccion del Medio Ambiente Tarija (PROMETA) works only in the Tarija area with the Tariquia Reserve as its main project. The National Service for Protected Areas (SERNAP) was created in 1998 as an independent operative structure connected to the Ministry of Sustainable Development, which overlooks most projects in Bolivia. The Fundacion Amigos de la Naturaleza (FAN) was founded in 1988 as a non-profit organization based in Santa Cruz; its most important project is the Noel Kempff Mercado National Park, where the carbon credits produced by the park's jungle are sold to international corporations. The Asociacion Boliviana Para la Conservacion (TROPICO) works with Parks in Peril, a branch of Nature Conservancy, an American group. TROPICO was established in 1986 by a group of professionals interested mostly in Eduardo Avaroa National Andean Reserve, which includes part of Uyuni Salt Flats. Parks Watch-Bolivia, legally incorporated in 2005, focusses on seven protected areas of the Madidi–Amboró Biological Corridor and works closely with SERNAP.

Ecotropica, a Brazilian ecology organization, has purchased and placed into protection thousands of acres of land in the Pantanal, the world's largest wetland and one of the richest ecosystems. The wetlands include 130,000 square kilometres (50,000 square miles) of the Rio Paraguay's floodplain in Bolivia, Paraguay and Brazil. The area is also under the protection of Ramsar, named after a town in Iran where the Convention on Wetlands of International Importance was first held. One hundred and fifty-four countries, including Bolivia, have pledged to protect 1,636 wetland sites important to waterfowl. The World Wildlife Fund is also involved with some of these organizations in specific projects.

Bolivia signed the Convention of International Trades in Endangered Species (CITES) of Wild Fauna and Flora treaty in October 1979. The treaty is a voluntary agreement to ensure international trade in endangered species does not threaten their survival. Trade of endangered species is monitored by a licensing system that protects 5,000 mammalian species and 28,000 plant species worldwide.

Bolivia's largest conservation focus is Noel Kempff Mercado National Park, formed in 1979 and designated a UNESCO preserve in 2000. The park includes 1,523,446 hectares of tropical rain forests, flooded savannahs, thorn scrub, dry forests, a huge wetland and the Huanchaca. Sometimes called Caparu Plateau, the Huanchaca is 344,000 hectares (850,000 acres) of Precambrian sandstone that has been carved into a fantasyland by both wind and water. From this plateau three dramatic waterfalls tumble over the ancient rock, which has been stained a reddish-brown by early plant forms. The roots of jungle vegetation cling to every open space.

Because of Noel Kempff's varied environments, isolation and size, there are 620 species of resident and migratory birds, 300 species of mammals and 2,700 species of plants recorded and classified. Biologists believe that there are probably about 4,000 plant species altogether. The mammals include about 1,000 giant river otters, a tenth of the world's entire population.

Noel Kempff has an operating budget of US$600,000 per year, 20 percent of which is obtained from a $1.5 million endowment fund. Recently the park and surrounding communities have received $25 million for the sale of carbon credits, a program initiated by the World Bank under the Kyoto Protocol and, in Bolivia, sponsored by American Power and Electric Corp, Pacificorp and British Petroleum Amoco. This means the international companies get 50 percent of the carbon credits produced by the park. The projected cost is $11 million, of which $2.2 million must be provided by Bolivia.

It is believed the trees will suck up 18.2 million tons of carbon over 30 years. While the experiment is in progress, locals who have lost income because of logging restrictions are receiving some of the money to help them switch to sustainable employment projects.

Since the initiation of the Noel Kempff carbon credit project, FAN has expanded to include under their wing the Rios Blanco Y Negro Reserve and Amboro National Park.

Zoos and More Parks

With almost 20 percent of the total landmass in reserves and parks, there is no end of possibilities for eco-tourism, with wildlife and cultural history being the two biggest attractions.

Madidi National Park and Chalalan Lodge both opened after the Yossi Ghinsberg story came out. Foreigners really wanted to experience traditional life in the jungle, even for just a few days. The community leaders of San José de Uchupiamonas realized that transporting tourists was more lucrative than taking agricultural products eight hours downriver to market. With the technical assistance of Conservation International and loans from the

Capybara like to wallow in mud and wiggle their ears and are the world's largest guinea pigs, weighing about 55 kilograms (120 pounds) when mature.

Inter-American Development Bank, the park was established and the lodge was built in traditional Tacana Nation style.

Animals, too, are protected, although the zoo in La Paz is in need of updating. Near Cochabamba, Juan Carlos founded the Comunidad Inti Wara Yassi (CIWY), an NGO with which England's Quest Overseas has worked since 2003. CIWY originated with Juan Carlos, a teacher at a trade school for orphans. He occasionally took his students on field trips to different cities and parks. During one excursion, they saw a burned rain forest with injured and starving birds, so Juan Carlos decided to dedicate CIWY to rehabilitating injured birds and animals. The foundation works out of Cochabamba in the Tunari Park area, where tourists can donate their vacation time to working and living at the centre.

A proposed pipeline going through the Kaa Lya del Gran Chaco National Park, established in 1995, has created another huge struggle in the preservation of traditional lifestyles. Conservationists are attempting to work with both Gas Trans Boliviano and Capitania del Alto y Bajo Izozog (CABI), a local indigenous group, to maintain the lifestyle of the isolated Guarani-Izoceño peoples. Their hope lies in CABI's upstanding reputation; in 2001 the organization won Spain's Bartolome de las Casas award for its environmental efforts.

But parks and isolated preserves are in danger. In addition to loggers and poachers, Bolivians have to hold land speculators, trophy hunters, cattle ranchers and mining, oil, and gas companies at bay in order to keep the areas safe. There is little financial help from the government and little money for the enforcement of land use laws and resource regulations.

Landscape Tourism

Beyond Bolivia's huge parks seething with wildlife, travellers will find plenty of other interesting destinations and extreme landscapes. The Uyuni Salt Flats, with the largest salt lake in the world, is a four-day excursion like nothing else on the planet. Not only is the scenery stunning and the bird life abundant, but the area is pristine and wonderfully devoid of any defined roads—just a funky narrow gauge rail line running along one edge. The experience of watching life progress in this isolated and bleak landscape is

The Salar de Uyuni is the largest salt lake in the world, covering over 12,000 square kilometres.

educating and refreshing, and the natural kindness displayed by the locals is a pleasure.

A less serene activity is a trip along the Road of Death. So dubbed by the Inter-American Development Bank, the Road of Death has killed an average of 200 people a year since 1935, when Paraguayan prisoners from the Chaco War built it as a transport route. The latest thrill is for bike-riding tourists to clutch their hand brakes while skidding 100 kilometres (60 miles) from El Cumbre (at 4,300 metres, or 14,100 feet above sea level) down to Coroico, which is at about 1,200 metres (4,000 feet). Near the end of the route, a brilliant entrepreneur offers beer with straws because the riders' hands are too sore from gripping the brakes to lift a bottle or glass. On the way down, cyclists watch as traffic drives on the opposite side of the road; this is so that down-going drivers can see how close to the edge of the cliff their wheels are as they pass those going up, hugging the mountain wall. Occasionally drivers misjudge and plunge over the edge—indicated by the numerous memorial shrines along the road. In 2006, a new road complete with tunnels was opened between Caravani, just beyond Coroico, and La Paz, leaving the Road of Death to slow-moving traffic and foreign cyclists. Even with decreased traffic the hazards still remain;

in 2007, a Canadian man was cycling and careened off the cliff to his death. Because the cool mountain air meets the steamy jungle heat at about 800 to 1,000 metres (2,500–3,000 feet), a mist slicks the muddy road and may be a contributing factor to accidents. For adventurers, this is a can't-miss trip. Just be certain to rent a bike from a reputable company, and check the brakes.

On the Road of Death, a descending vehicle must drive along the edge so the driver can see how close his wheels are to the edge. Upcoming traffic gets to hug the mountain.

The Chacaltaya Ski Resort is the oldest ski resort in South America, and, at 5,300 metres (17,400 feet), it's also the highest in the world. Indians refuse to go to Chacaltaya (which means "cold" in Aymara) because in the 1930s an avalanche killed the engineer building the lift. Today, the bad luck is more focussed on the mountain itself—the glacier is melting quickly, shortening the ski run. As much as 80 percent of the glacier has disappeared in the last 15 years, and the rest will be gone by 2015. (So get going!) Ski season is from February to April, but hiking on the mountain is year-round.

If skiing isn't your thing, you can climb Huayna Potosi just across the way from Chacaltaya. The 6,000-metre (20,000-foot) mountain is said to be one of the easiest high-altitude climbs in the world. And if "easy" isn't your thing, the peak to conquer may be Sajama, towering at 6,542 metres (21,500 feet) above sea level and shadowing a bleak ancient village where electricity has yet to arrive. Sajama is also home to the highest forest of Queñua trees in the world. The gnarled species, with its tiny leaves and red bark, grows along the mountain slopes as high as 5,200 metres (17,000 feet). Hot springs dot the landscape just south of the village and a lake to the north is frequented by herds of vicuña and rheas. The mountain has also given scientists a 25,000-year-old ice core to study.

For something a little less exerting, grab a reed boat or kayak and paddle the highest navigable lake in the world, Lake Titicaca, where you might spot Bolivia's land-locked navy. Or grab some clubs and visit La Paz's golf course, where crawling from hole to hole is a challenge due to the lack of oxygen at that elevation.

If oxygen is your thing, the trails out of Sorata start at around 2,150 metres (7,000 feet) and follow old gold and rubber trade routes down into the Amazon. This is where Colonel Fawcett, the British adventurer, started to pursue the legend of El Dorado.

To end this history before the beginning, I recommend you plan a stop travelling back into Bolivian pre-history: the dinosaur tracks at Cal Orck'o, just out of Sucre. There are a number of trackways at the site, with at least 5,000 prints dating from the cretaceous period (about 70 million years ago). The slanting slab, located in a gravel pit, includes prints from sauropods, theropods and ornithopods. According to Swiss paleontologist Christian Meyer, these are the greatest dinosaur tracks in the world, covering an area of 25,000 square metres (270,000 square feet). One unbroken set extends for 350 metres (1,150 feet), and another rare set suggests that the animal that made the prints was walking very quickly. Also found were two dino eggs, about 25 and 40 centimetres (10 and 16 inches) in diameter, and one leg bone.

Conclusion

My love for Bolivia began during my first visit, when I travelled up the Madeira River from Manaus, Brazil. On arriving home, I couldn't get the country and its people out of my mind. I convinced Kim Andre from Hunter Publishing in the US that a guidebook to Bolivia would make them a fortune. She believed me and in 2003, my husband and I returned to spend six months experiencing and ferreting out every hidden corner of the country.

We found that Bolivia offered even more than we imagined: wildlife enthusiasts can see the largest group of wild macaws in the world nesting just outside of Trinidad, and freshwater dolphins will nuzzle up to you as you wade or paddle in Amazonian rivers. The museums and galleries are up to international standards and jam-packed with treasures that can keep museum buffs going for days. The cities are loaded with good restaurants and jazz bars, clean hotels and interesting plazas. I can't stay away from Thelonius's Jazz Bar and La Rencon Restaurant in La Paz, or the Camba Steak House in Santa Cruz. If "big-city travel" isn't for you, follow the webs of Inca roads throughout the countryside or visit Kallawaya medicine men practising ancient cures in the remote Apolobamba region. And even with the parade of political goons who have caused so much turmoil in Bolivia, the people are still patient and friendly. They will smile at foreigners' funny accents and are always eager to show tourists their wares, whether it's a sack of coca leaves or a bag of tasty *salteñas* (the best kind have quail eggs inside). One night in La Paz, my husband and I sat on our hotel balcony overlooking the city, in complete awe of Bolivia and marvelling over the incredible experiences we'd had. The country is such a multicoloured rainbow of landscapes, cultures, people, foods and adventures. We agreed that if anything ever happened to Canada, we'd immigrate to Bolivia. But go and experience it for yourself, and let me know what you think. As they say in Bolivia,

Que le vaya bien.

Go well.

Sources and Recommended Reading

Anderson, Jon Lee. *Che*. New York: Grove Press, 1997. (This tome was extensively researched and includes exclusive family interviews. Although it's over 800 pages, it's a fast read.)

Anderson, Scott and Jon Lee. *Inside the League*. New York: Dodd Mead, June 1986. (Covers some of the Operation Condor period of Latin America.)

Arnade, Charles. *Bolivian History*. La Paz: Los Amigos del Libro, 1984. (Although it is obvious English is the second language of the author, his knowledge is commendable.)

Cramer, Mark. *Culture Shock!* Portland, Oregon: Graphic Arts Center Publishing Co., 1996. (This is an excellent little book with interesting tidbits on how to survive while travelling in Bolivia. It summarizes the political history with hilarious yet sound advice. Most helpful are the descriptions of words like *Cholla, pollera* and *chicha*.)

Fawcett, Brian. *Exploration Fawcett*. London: Companion Book Club, 1954. (Colonel Fawcett's manuscripts arranged and edited by his son. This is an excellent reconstruction of the famous explorer's trips.)

Garcia Márquez, Gabriel. *The General in His Labyrinth*. Trans. Edith Grossman. New York: Alfred A. Knopf, 1990. (A Nobel Prize winner's novel about Simón Bolívar's last months.)

Ghinsberg, Yossi. *Back from Tuichi*. New York: Random House, 1993. (The story of an Israeli tourist who nearly died on an adventurous river trip; a parade of Israelis followed in his shoes.)

Guise, Anselm Verener Lee. *Six Years in Bolivia*. Ashland, Ohio: Purdue University Press, 1997. (First published in 1922, this reprint is written by a mining engineer working and travelling through the country.)

Klein, Herbert S. *A Concise History of Bolivia*. Cambridge, UK: Cambridge University Press, 2003. (This is the definitive post-colonial history, with the clearest analyses on the market.)

Masur, Gerhard. *Simón Bolívar*. Albuquerque: University of New Mexico Press, 1948 and 1969. (This book covers every aspect of Bolívar's life from birth to death. A great read.)

Métraux, Alfred. *The History of the Incas*. New York: Schocken Books, 1970. (This history combines archeological, anthropological and cultural finds in its descriptions of the Inca people.)

Morales, Waltraud Q. *A Brief History of Bolivia*. New York: Checkmark Books, 2004. (For some interesting details about modern history.)

Morgan, Ted. *An Uncertain Hour*. New York: William Morrow & Co., 1990. (A well-researched tale of Klaus Barbie, his life in Lyon and his trial.)

Powers, William. *Whispering in the Giant's Ear.* New York: Bloomsbury Publishing, 2006. (This is mainly about Noel Kempff National Park, with diversions to other important ecological sights in Bolivia. It's told as both a travel story and a description of working in Bolivia.)

Santos, Rosario, ed. *Fat Man from La Paz.* New York: Seven Stories Press, 2000. (These fiction stories give a good look at contemporary life behind the travel scene in Bolivia. One story in particular, about the Chaco War, is a must-read.)

Young, Rusty and Thomas McFadden. *Marching Powder.* New York: St. Martin's Griffin, 2004. (A gripping tale of life in La Paz's San Pedro Prison.)

Sources and Recommended Reading

Index

About the Author

Born in Winnipeg in 1943, **Vivien Lougheed** was raised by her Polish-Romanian grandparents who instilled within her a desire for adventure. From her home base of Prince George she has travelled extensively throughout British Columbia, China, Pakistan, the Mediterranean, Central and South America, Africa and the Himalayas of Tibet and Nepal. In her first book, *Central America by Chickenbus* (1986), she all but coined the term that is now synonymous with local transportation and travelling on the cheap. Since then she has written more than ten books including *Kluane National Park Hiking Guide*, *Forbidden Mountains*, *From the Chilcotin to the Chilkoot: Selected Hikes of Northern BC* and *Tungsten John* (co-written with husband John Harris).